Jules Olitski

Distributed by New York Graphic Society   Greenwich, Connecticut

Jules Olitski   Museum of Fine Arts, Boston

Library of Congress catalog card no. 72-94431
ISBN 0-87846-070-5
Type set by Wrightson Typographers, Boston
Color engravings by Techno-colour Co. Inc., Montreal
Printed in Canada by Litho Associates, St. Laurent
Designed by Carl F. Zahn

Exhibition dates

Museum of Fine Arts, Boston
April 6 – May 13, 1973

Albright-Knox Art Gallery, Buffalo
May 31 – July 29, 1973

Whitney Museum of American Art, New York
September 7 – November 4, 1973

Photograph credits

Dawn Andrews: p. 26
Herbert G. Hamilton and Wayne O. Lemmon: cover and pp. 53, 57, 63
Karol Ike: pp. 29, 37, 49, 69, 71
Eric Pollitzer: pp. 8, 9, 10, 11, 12, 25, 27, 31, 39, 41, 43, 51, 55, 61, 65
David Scribner: p. 15 (right)
Frank J. Thomas: pp. 47, 67

Cover illustration:

48

3rd Indomitable, 1970 (detail)
Courtesy Lawrence Rubin Gallery, New York

Acknowledgments

We wish to thank the lenders for their generosity in allowing
their pictures to be shown in this exhibition. Also we are in-
debted to the artist himself, who has given generously of his
time. The same is true of Clement Greenberg. Others who have
helped to make this show a reality include Dawn Andrews,
William Agee, William Rubin, Elinor Woron, Betsy Cheek, and
James Lebron. The Lawrence Rubin Gallery, the Kasmin Gallery, the André Emmerich Gallery, and the David Mirvish Gallery
have all been extremely helpful with regard both to the preparation of the catalogue and the organization of the show.
Finally, special acknowledgment should be given to the Visiting
Committee of the Department of Contemporary Art, without
whose support this exhibition would not be possible.

K.M.

This project is supported by a grant from the
National Endowment for the Arts in Washington, D.C.,
a Federal Agency

Contents

Introduction

by Kenworth Moffett

I

Over the past two or three years the painting of Jules Olitski has begun to seem decisive. For a surprising number of younger painters he is like a block, *the* influence that has to be gone through or overcome if any fundamental innovation or breakthrough is to be achieved.[1] This is the position that Pollock's art occupied in the 1950's, though never quite so explicitly or self-consciously. What is special and even ominous is that some of the most mature and genuinely original painters of our time have found themselves running into Olitski's innovations.

Aside from the sheer quality and phenomenal consistency of quality of his work, this situation has to do, I think, with two facts, the first contingent and stylistic, the second deeper and more fundamental. First, Olitski is the artist who has explored the painterly (or "das Malerische") — the idiom that has dominated Western painting since the Renaissance — during the 1960's, a period when picturemaking was moving in the opposite direction. Now that the nonpainterly seems exhausted, at least temporarily, and more and more painters are turning to looser handling, Olitski finds himself in the lead.

But more essentially, it is Olitski who has developed and revised Jackson Pollock's central innovation, the allover picture, in order to make it serve color. In so doing he has drawn radical and far-reaching conclusions about the nature of the abstract picture — conclusions that have taken on an inescapable authority.

1
Larry Poons has acknowledged his debt to Olitski, and Walter Darby Bannard has written that Olitski "has preempted serious new painting. He is for the time being our best painter" ("Quality, Style and Olitski," *Artforum*, vol. 11 [October 1972], p. 67). In a mock-bitter mood Dan Christensen called Olitski "the monster" after seeing his 1972 show in New York.

II

When Olitski first began studying at the National Academy, he already showed a predilection for the painterly; his portraits of this time manifest a love of rich handling and of Rembrandtesque subtleties of chiaroscuro. And it was at the National Academy that he learned the full range of the old masters' devices — scumbling, glazes, impasto — which he continues to use today.

But soon Olitski found that he had to unlearn this painting culture — unlearn it in order to discover its relevance for modernist art. Thus it was that, when he finally turned to abstract painting in the late 1940's, while living in Paris and working under great personal stress, it was as an effort at abnegation. Feeling oppressed by what seemed to him a too fully assimilated training, Olitski began to ask what all that he had learned had to do with him, with his own feelings. He stopped visiting museums. He began to paint blindfolded, a device that had already been employed by certain Surrealist artists in the effort to escape their own expectations and assumptions: the learned habits of hand and eye. Although the results of Olitski's blindfold painting were not especially distinguished, these pictures did have a liberating effect on him, personally and artistically. Notwithstanding his deep loyalties to the old masters, he was now willing to risk everything to discover his artistic self.

After returning from Europe, Olitski essayed another novel approach to picture making, one that now seems prophetic. Searching out used drawing boards in art schools, he brought them back to his studio and copied them or, as Olitski himself describes it, painted "portraits" of them. Seen as a painting, a used drawing board is a picture from which the drawing has been removed. The center, the traditional locus of meaning and importance, is blank, negative, while lines and markings, the result of strokes running off the paper placed on the board, appear only at the edges, creating an internal frame.

Eschewing spectral colors in reaction against the bright, Fauvelike hues he had employed in his Paris years, Olitski next began a series of paintings that were the reverse of the drawing board "portraits" but no less prophetic. Thick, plastered areas of white impasto swell up out of the center of grayed and generally heavily painted surfaces. The whole has a viscous density far exceeding the normal facture of oil painting. Sometimes these paintings are reminiscent of landscape or even more of a Rembrandt portrait, where the thickest impasto coincides with both the approximate center of the picture and the area of greatest highlight. In the way that the delicate, neutral tonalities and earth colors transform the aggressive relieflike paint matter, these paintings remind one of postwar European painting: Fautrier, Dubuffet, and de Staël.[2] In any event they are very French and out of the mainstream of American abstraction as it was developing in those years.

2
See Lawrence Alloway in the catalogue *Matter Painting,* London, Institute of Contemporary Art, 1960.

An indication of Olitski's affinities with the *belle peinture* tradition, these "impasto pictures," with their subtleties of chiaroscuro and sensuous paint handling, point forward to his most recent work. More importantly, they are already of surprisingly high quality.

In 1960 Olitski made an abrupt shift in style that suddenly aligned his art with what was then the most advanced American painting. His canvases became larger, and their surfaces were stripped bare of impasto or paint texture of any kind; prismatic colors appeared in the form of bright, biomorphic-looking shapes with sharp, undulating contours usually placed off-center on a black ground. Undoubtedly, Olitski had been decisively affected by the stain painters, Morris Louis and Kenneth Noland, whose pictures, like his, had been chosen by Clement Greenberg for exhibition at French & Co. Yet Olitski's change was not quite as dramatic as it might appear: he had already insinuated bright colors into his last impasto paintings, and the new pictures, like the ones immediately previous, showed areas of light emerging from a dark ground.

Still, this was a different kind of painting — a painting that had little to do with tone or variations of value per se, let alone relieflike effects, but a great deal to do with contour, placement, and color as hue. Unlike Louis and Noland, who thinned their paint to achieve a watercolorlike airiness, Olitski was searching for a kind of paint application that, without impasto, would continue to evoke density and fullness. It was this intention, I think, that lay behind his experimentation with different paint media, many of which turned out to be impermanent, or else produced flat, posterlike surfaces with an opaque, brittle look.

Drawing Board Echo, 1952, oil on wood, 30″ x 30″
Courtesy Lawrence Rubin Gallery, New York

Drawing Board, 1951–1952, oil on board, 30" x 25"
Courtesy Lawrence Rubin Gallery, New York

These difficulties induced Olitski's turn, late in 1961, to the kind of staining then already seen in Frankenthaler, Dzubas, Noland, and Louis: thinned pigment that would soak through the canvas fabric and not lie inertly on the surface. He also followed these artists in using areas of bare canvas to intensify the identification of color and support by stressing the lack of textural change between painted and unpainted areas. Color seemed disembodied, optical, light, and airy.

Olitski's paintings of 1962 and 1963 also relate to the work of Louis and Noland in their hard-edged, imposing, holistic design, which is laterally expansive and non-Cubist in feeling. Back-and-forth space is suppressed by the elimination of overlapping, and alignment with the rectilinear frame is made ambiguous by the use of exclusively rounded forms, usually organized around a central core.[3]

On the other hand, Louis, with his floods and rivulets of paint, and Noland, with his geometric bands and maskings, both sought out impersonal, unobtrusive sorts of edges so as to give even greater primacy to color. Olitski emphasizes irregular, explicitly drawn cutting lines, which charge the negative areas with life and evoke the sculptural. The latter effect is reinforced by the rich, dense, velvety surfaces, achieved by rubbing the paint in with a sponge, and the crowding, jostling, interlocking shapes.

Together with what are usually opposing primaries and sharp value changes, the effect subordinates pure color to the force and vigor of dramatic design.[4] Olitski succeeds magnificently in the best of these pictures, which are his first truly major, original works; and he succeeds despite the fact that he is working against the logic of stain, as it were. It appears that he wants a certain sculptural body and density, while staining pushes the picture in the direction of a more purely optical life.

In a way these pictures are more radical than those of the other stain painters, or rather they led to something more radical. Since painting's theoretical self-consciousness first emerged in the sixteenth century, it had been recognized that there was an inherent conflict between drawing and color—a conflict that manifested itself in different "schools" and, in any case, demanded compromise and subordination. Modernist art broaches no such compromises, and Olitski, by driving both the optical and the sculptural to extreme limits in these pictures, further isolated the age-old issue. And it was exactly the isolation of this conflict that permitted Olitski's next step: to opt for pure color and banish contour drawing. Henceforth the full expressive force of that kind of drawing will appear solely in Olitski's *sculpture.* It is as if he can now realize his gifts as a draftsman and as a colorist only in separate media.

3
Olitski has always shown a preference for elliptical, circular forms, either concentric or in figure eights, and in terms of actual influence Noland's concentric circles only reinforced an already existing inclination. On the other hand Louis and Noland certainly influenced Olitski with their use of stain and also with the hard-edged design that distinguishes their works from the softer contours favored by Frankenthaler and Dzubas. It was Noland who first discovered that staining softens the effect of a hard edge while the latter in turn flattens and tautens the softness of staining.

4
For an excellent discussion of these paintings see Michael Fried, "New York Letter," *Art International,* vol. 8 (March 1964), pp. 40–42.

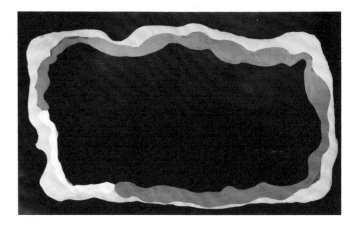

Untitled, c. 1960, oil-miscible acrylic on canvas, 80⅞" x 135"
Courtesy Lawrence Rubin Gallery, New York

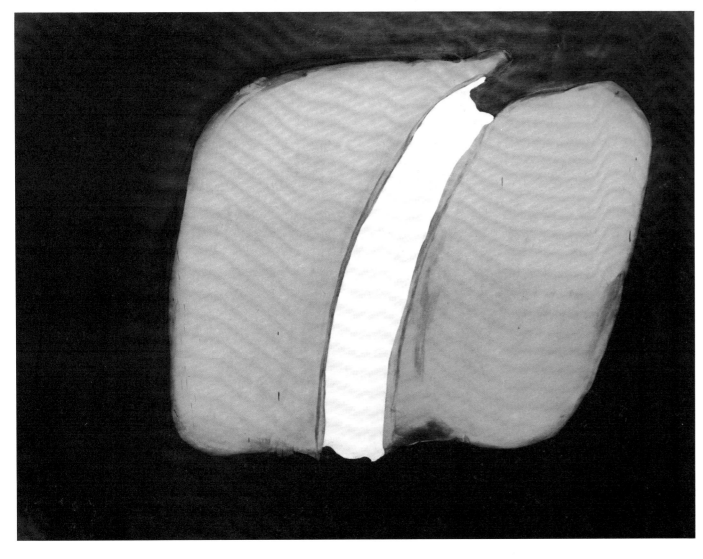

Osculum Silence, 1960, dye on canvas, 80" x 108"
Courtesy Lawrence Rubin Gallery, New York.

Potsy, 1960, oil-miscible acrylic on canvas, 80" x 68¼"
Courtesy Lawrence Rubin Gallery, New York

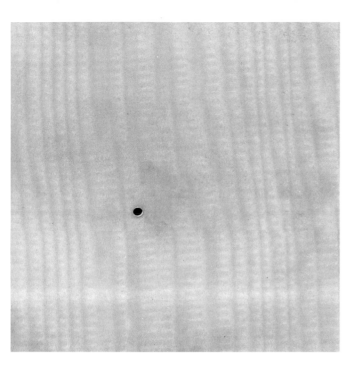

V, 1963, oil-miscible acrylic on canvas, 64″ x 64″
Courtesy Lawrence Rubin Gallery, New York

One might say that the history of Western art is repeating itself in reverse. The tremulously responsive curving line that can take the eye back and around objects in depth first entered painting as a two-dimensional equivalent of sculpture. Abstract painting in general and Olitski in particular now seem to be forcing it back into three dimensions where, at least in Olitski's sculpture, it continues to have a marked pictorial character.

All this begins to happen in pictures like *Fatal Plunge Lady,* where a flood of color rolls downward toward the bottom edge without quite achieving it. Finally, in 1964 the flow comes to dominate the entire center of the picture, crowding up against margins of raw canvas or swatches and spottings of color at the very edges.

Thanks to the paint application (with sponges but mostly rollers) and the still slightly sculptural edgings that occur at the margins of the field, pictures such as *Flaubert Red* and *Deep Drag* feel full and dense, packed with color.[5] They represent Olitski's first major "breakthrough," which is primarily one of composition. The picture consists of a single spread of color with drawing and changes of color and value relegated to the perimeters.

Although a group of masterworks resulted from this layout, one feels that Olitski did not exhaust its possibilities. Instead, he moved quickly in the following year to deal with two new issues. As can be seen in pictures like *Hot Ticket* and *Tin Lizzy Green,* he still wished to introduce sharp changes of hue within the field, especially complementary changes from, say, green to red, a difficult thing to achieve by staining without disruptive grayed or muddied transitional areas.

This was one of the two considerations that led Olitski to what should be seen as his second breakthrough: the spray technique. Spraying meant broken color, tiny drops that lay side by side, fused in the eye or on the surface; modulation of color into color became less disruptive and smoother.

In an abstract painting, in which the materials themselves used in their literal immediacy come to count more and more as the sole expressive agents, the discovery of a new technique, a new manner of application, is tantamount to a whole new style and feeling; often a response to specific problems, it usually turns out to have wider implications. This was true, for example, of Jackson Pollock's drip technique, Morris Louis' stainings, and more recently of Larry Poons' pourings; and it is true of Olitski's spraying.

What is meant here by new "style" is perhaps best explained by pointing to the fact that spraying meant a new kind of color picture, one that was closer, say, to Louis' veils than to Olitski's own previous stain pictures, or to those of Noland, or to Louis' "unfurleds" or "stripes." The latter sort of color picture might be called "Fauve," having emerged full-blown first in the work of Matisse and the Fauves. But the initial impetus had come from Van Gogh, Gauguin, and Cézanne. Cézanne had introduced a system of color values as a way to restore to painting a dramatic, intense articulation while continuing to offer Impressionist color. The Fauves abstracted his system still further in an effort to heighten coloristic impact; instead of dividing a surface into planes of color, they made a single hue stand for the whole local color of an object.

5
Kermit S. Champa, "Olitski: Nothing but Color," *Art News,* vol. 66 (March 1967), p. 74.

In the Fauve kind of picture the color effect is first of all one of contrast resulting from the juxtaposition of frank, pure, discrete hues, all more or less clearly separated. Sharp differences of value inherent in different hues at full intensity (e.g., blue with yellow) are accepted for the sake of the vigor and optical energy that their contrast evokes. Far brighter and far more obviously colorful than the paintings of the Impressionists, the Fauve pictures stress declarative immediacy and the individual identity of each hue. White is often included to heighten and help unify an optical dazzle; and light seems to bounce off or be reflected from the picture rather than, as with Impressionism, being located within it. Such pictures live by vivid, ringing complementaries or else by unexpected juxtapositions. (Matisse and, among abstract painters, Kenneth Noland have been masters of this side-by-side type of color invention.)

The difficulties here are those of unity, for the separate hues must be kept from canceling each other out and creating an effect that the Germans call *bunt*. The most frequent solution, evident in the work of Matisse as well as in the stained paintings of Louis and Noland, has been to give clear dominance to one color in terms of area size or else to resort to a generous use of white.[6] In 1964 Olitski made these two solutions fully explicit by exaggerating them in pictures like *Flaubert Red* on the one hand and *Monkey Woman* on the other.

6
An alternative solution is, of course, to close-value the whole picture as Noland has often done.
It is interesting to note that Matisse and the Fauves also followed Cézanne in leaving exposed relatively large primed and sized areas of white canvas. Morris Louis' "unfurleds" are a classic example of this type of Fauve solution.

Since juxtaposed hues at full intensity bring with them clear edges and emphatic design, the colorist of the Fauve type can only maintain the primacy of color by preventing his design from taking on an inert, filled-in look, from seeming merely posterlike and graphic. Also, since the eye first grasps differences of light and dark, he must so organize his picture that the sharp value changes present in full-intensity color do not balance out as value accents but retain their full force as hue. Noland and Louis often solved this problem by resorting to various kinds of symmetry, i.e., a design that more or less obviated compositional decisions after a certain point.

Olitski's spray technique tends toward a different kind of color picture, one that might be called "Impressionist," although it has been adumbrated in much earlier painting, especially in the seventeenth and eighteenth century. Here the interest is primarily in the kind of color experience that results from the subtle modulation of color into color across the surface. Sharp changes of hue and value and also drawing — anything that will interrupt the continuous movement of color — are de-emphasized. Usually, this has meant some kind of painterly application that results in broken color, such as the Impressionist touch, or Louis' layerings, or Olitski's spray.

The Impressionist picture tends toward density and warmth as it also tends toward middle grayness and an initial monochromatic look; coloristic richness emerges only gradually. Overall tonality dominates, and changes of hue issue as fugitive, suggestive, evanescent, and nuanced. Because of the radically reduced value range, slight color shifts appear as identical with equally slight value shifts. The emphasis is not on the identity of individual hues but on a single, richly varied chromatic substance informed by an absorbent, inner light.

One Time, 1964, enamel paint on canvas, 82″ x 69¼″
Courtesy Lawrence Rubin Gallery, New York

Since the Impressionist type of color picture develops across the surface, the artist is not forced to continually step back to balance out his composition, as was often the case with the Fauve painters; on the other hand his main difficulties are those of accentuation and variety, of introducing sharp, pungent changes of hue or value, or both. A secondary problem is of stopping the flow, of turning his field into a picture.

A motif drawn from nature helped the Impressionists to deal with the problems of accentuation and pictorial completeness.[7] Olitski's solution to both of these problems resulted from his manner of application and from his discovery of the different nature of the margins of a flat, more or less uniformly accented abstract picture and its center; so, for example, with a few marks or strokes at the edges he has been able to introduce what are often abrupt, Fauvelike bursts of hue and value while simultaneously delimiting and declaring his sprayed fields as self-contained pictorial units.[8]

Along with the problem of color fusion, the second consideration that led Olitski to spraying has to do with the creation of a new surface.

All modernist pictures since Cubism orient themselves to flatness as their principle of unity; their success depends first of all upon a felt continuity between the illusion and the resistant plane surface.[9] Expressively, this conveys a taut immediacy, which modernist sensibility finds especially exhilarating. As the materials of painting have increasingly taken on a more exclusive role in the final effect, flatness has become more assertive. Since World War II there has been a tendency toward ways of working and paint applications that in and of themselves declare flatness through the palpably material literalness of the whole surface, a flatness that must contrive an illusion commensurate with itself.

A complicating factor here has been the growing emphasis on color during this same period. The new flatness makes a strong tactile appeal, pure color an exclusively optical one. A central problem for the abstract color painter, then, is to somehow unite optical illusion and tactile surface, to render them continuous. The solution, especially when the color field is broad and uninterrupted, lies primarily with paint consistency and application.[10]

7
By painting in close values and by creating an equalized surface tension, with every square inch receiving the same emphasis, the Impressionists automatically achieved a very cohesive unity. Hence they were not interested in composition per se or in its formal elaboration; they gave attention to tonal recession but not to compositional accents. They did not really compose but chose scenes that composed themselves, that gave a merely sufficient sense of completeness, such as a centered road that led back into perspective or a view that mirrored itself in the reflecting surface of water.
On the question of the relation between accentuation and nature in the Impressionist picture see Clement Greenberg, "The Late Monet," in Art and Culture, Boston, Beacon Press, 1961, pp. 37–45.

8
The delimiting function of these marks has been stressed by Darby Bannard in "Quality, Style and Olitski," pp. 64–67.

9
It has been one of Clement Greenberg's main contributions to the interpretation of modern art that he has indicated and stressed this point. See, for example, "Collages," in Art and Culture, pp. 70–83.

10
This point was imperfectly grasped by Barnett Newman, who flattened his color fields with vertical bands. His rectilinear design does not directly affect the field, however; it merely implies flatness by frontality, by referring the interior to the shape of the support. Newman's fields are often ambivalent or at least unemphatic in their flatness, for the illusion and the surface are not explicitly continuous.

Staining, by identifying disembodied color with the threaded wovenness of the canvas fabric, automatically recreates the new modernist flatness. And painters working with stain have often strengthened this inherent property of their technique by leaving areas of bare canvas, making explicit the identity of color and canvas texture. (To further strengthen tactility, stain painters have sometimes teased and scrubbed their surfaces to get a rich, velvety or suedelike texture, or mixed agents like pearlessence into the pigments.) When fully covered with positive color, the canvas weave becomes less a factor in the final effect.

In Olitski's paintings of 1964 a single hue threatens to cover the entire surface. To give a sense of expansion and of internal delimitedness and to declare the identification of color and canvas, he left areas of raw canvas at the margins. This meant edges that in turn affected the character of the field. As Olitski later wrote, "Edge is drawing and drawing is always *on* the surface. The color areas take on the appearance of overlay, and if the conception of form is governed by edge—no matter how successfully it possesses the surface—paint, even when stained into raw canvas, remains on or above the surface. I think, on the contrary, of color as being *in,* not *on* the surface."[11]

Sprayed color meant a new kind of tactile density that did not depend on edge. As Clement Greenberg has observed, "The grainy surface Olitski creates with his way of spraying is a new kind of paint surface. It offers tactile associations hitherto foreign, more or less, to picture-making; and it does new things with color. Together with color, it contrives an illusion of depth back to the picture's surface; it is as if that surface, in all its literalness, were enlarged to contain a world of color and light differentiations impossible to flatness but which yet manages not to violate flatness."[12]

One might say that the sculptural appeal Olitski had eliminated in the form of contour drawing now reasserted itself as the literally sculptural or tactile. So, too, it asserted itself as shading, yet shading not attached to an edge or plane but identical with the development of color. By spraying paint unevenly, Olitski achieves different paint densities, which automatically result in light and dark shifts; and, again thanks to spraying, these shifts can be very finely graded. In this way Olitski reintroduced traditional chiaroscuro with all of its associations of richness and mystery into the abstract picture. Color in these pictures can seem deceptively gorgeous and ingratiating. At times Olitski, like Monet before him, appears to be testing the modernist tolerance for sheer beauty. But these lovely hues and softly suggestive depths are somehow stiffened to the hard, resistant surface. An indulgent sensuousness and romanticism are tautened and withheld, transformed into something grand and sometimes sublime.

11
"Painting in Color", in *XXXIII International Biennial Exhibition of Art*, Venice, 1966, p. 39.

12
"Jules Olitski," in *XXXIII International Biennial Exhibition of Art*, p. 38. This grainy texture is the result of the combination of air and paint produced by a spray gun. If the canvas is unprimed, the air pressure blows up nap from the bare surface, which also counts in the final result. By varying the gun's distance from the canvas and the fineness of the burst, the artist can further alter this surface texture.

Born in Snovsk, 1963, oil-miscible acrylic on canvas, 132″ x 90″
Courtesy The Art Institute of Chicago,
Gift of The Ford Foundation

Honey, 1972, mild steel, 8′ diameter, 14″ high
Collection of the artist

The flattened textures of the early spray paintings were a way to affirm tactile surface and admit optical color. Nonetheless, these pictures too can be seen as calling for increased flatness because of the far more sensible illusion that spraying, like all painterly applications, evokes.[13] This is not something that hurts the quality of these pictures, which is for the most part extraordinary, but rather something that serves as a stimulus to further development. Around 1967 Olitski began to reaffirm a stronger sense of flatness by freighting his pigments with various elements such as gel or metallic agents so as to render them more viscous, hence more coarsely tactile or reflective.

In art the revision of one crucial variable implies an alteration of all the rest. A heavy, thick buildup of paint on the surface means literal density and opacity; it asks for its own kind of illusion of transparency and depth. Characteristically, Olitski found this by using, in addition to spraying, devices he had learned in the art schools and museums: blendings, scumbling, glazes, impasto, and varnish; painting as the old masters understood it: a complicated layered buildup of the literal depth of the surface in order to induce imaginative, pictorial depths; real opacity and transparency, which become illusive and suggestive. As was the case with the rich chiaroscuro that resulted from his sprayings, Olitski here repossesses a distinctive aspect of traditional painting culture.

If the increased tactility of his flattened, continuous surfaces is a result of Olitski's efforts to give a more taut unity of his color fields, it is also the result of a very personal artistic preference.

Unlike Kenneth Noland, who escapes the sculptural through expressive weightlessness, Olitski, as already noted, always seeks to retain something of the plastic fullness, the sculptural character of older painting. For this reason his most radical moves are often in the service of tradition, efforts to salvage for modernism the splendors of the past.

The dialectical interconnection between the conventions of painting also helps to explain the development of Olitski's color over the past six years. While many of the early sprayed pictures, especially those of 1965, continue to show dramatic changes of color (e.g., red to green), in the best of these paintings the effect is increasingly of a single, unifying color with perspicuous shifts occurring discretely, along with the marginings, only at the edges.

The more material and tactile Olitski's surfaces have become the more consistently do they display this monochromatic, general look. Only rarely do they offer prismatic hues; when these occur, it is usually in the guise of tints and shades. Most recently Olitski's pictures have even inclined toward neutrals and earth colors, something else that is a function of his coarser, declaratively tactile surfaces. Positive hues, like abrupt textural changes, can threaten the synthesis of tactile and optical; they can undermine the pictorial and approach colored bas-relief. But there are all sorts of variations and exceptions here; even a surprising degree of value change is sometimes permitted. Everything depends on the character of the paint surface and the way it is applied. Never has *matière* been quite so integral and decisive.[14]

13
Bannard, "Quality, Style and Olitski," p. 67.

14
Olitski uses an enormous variety of techniques in applying paint: hand, mitten, roller, broom, mop, etc. He also employs various methods to remove it: squeegees, scrapers, knives, etc.

The result is an extraordinary range of textural effects: caked, encrusted, hard and shiny, waxy, gritty, crumbly, grainy, milky, and ceramiclike. These surfaces both seduce and distance the viewer; and the same is true of their delicate, rare, exquisite hues; the sensuous delights and beauties of *belle peinture* with the impassiveness that belongs to the best of abstract painting.

There is a unique and highly cultivated aesthetic thrill in watching initial simplicity, even blankness, yield ultimate richness and fullness of experience.[15] Squeezing the viewer's reactions within a radically narrowed range, the new pictures challenge the viewer to connoisseurship.[16] Wisps of color and shading are always on the verge of congealing into a legible pattern, but before this can occur, the flux and shiftings begin again. The not-quite-graspable character, the suggestiveness and ambiguity are of a piece with those rare and fugitive hues that emerge only after sustained looking.

Extreme asymmetry of design and occult balance, highly refined, nuanced effects issuing from a pregnant "emptiness"—these are qualities we know from Far Eastern art; and that, too, is the product of a highly sophisticated and self-conscious, artistic culture like our own. In their painterly directness and amplitude, in their non-decorative involution and drama, Olitski's paintings remain part of the Western easel tradition, although, as I argue below, they hold a very special place at the extreme limit of this tradition.

15
For an insightful discussion of how Olitski's pictures work see Ken Carpenter "On Order in the Paintings of Jules Olitski," *Art International*, vol. 16 (December 1972), pp. 26–30.

16
So narrow is the range that it is almost impossible to distinguish between real shadows caused by relief on the surface, the implied shadows resulting from different paint densities, and, finally, the actual shadows caused by uneven lighting in the place where the picture hangs.

III

Attending to a picture aesthetically, that even distribution of detached attention by means of which the viewer savors the wholeness and unity of a painting, is a matter of suspending practical seeing in favor of the world's surface. It represents an alteration of normal, purposive looking by letting the visual field Itself structure what is seen. Vision is spread equally and thus tends toward the flat and optical, with the areas between objects becoming as important as the objects themselves. From time immemorial every painter must have taken up this mental attitude by narrowing his eyes, or stepping back from his work, when he wished to assess the overall distribution of visual weights.

Impressionism, which was a dissolving of Naturalism into aestheticism, revolutionized painting by assuming this attitude *toward nature;* that is to say, the Impressionists sought, insofar as it was possible, an identification of the visual field and the pictorial surface. Hence their interest in optical color. The attempt was made to see everything as if the eye were equidistant from it (the so-called far vision). Because their approach (working primarily in close values with neutralized brushstrokes, each approximately of the same size and shape) guaranteed such an evenly accented and homogeneous surface, they were able to work across the surface without continually stepping back.

Undermining this, however, were perspective and the structure of reality. By isolating the visual field as a whole, the Impressionists had made surface and depth, at least potentially, discontinuous. Even in Monet's *Lily Pads,* a motif chosen because it easily aligned itself with the surface, the identification remains incomplete, since Monet still had to deal with a foreground and a background, both of which asked for a different kind of articulation.[17] The visual and pictorial fields were always to remain in conflict so long as the structure of reality had to be accommodated; the breaking of this structure in favor of the surface was, of course, the task of Cubism.

Fauvism eliminated Impressionist evenness in favor of a hierarchy of accents — the traditional stepping back and balancing out. From this point of view Fauvism was conservative; but the problem it threw up, that of avoiding decoration by relating forms across a flattened surface, eventually drove the Cubists to their radical step of subverting perspective and the autonomy of objects. Nature was no longer chosen for the sake of two-dimensionality but was adapted to it. The essential means to achieve this adaptation were rectilinear drawing and *passage,* the disassociation of contour from interior shading.

17
It is perhaps for this reason that Monet had more consistent success with motifs like *Wisteria* and *Irises*, flowers against the sky, where everything could be handled as parallel to the picture plane.

Seeking the directness and explicitness of sharp edges, Mondrian dispensed with *passage* and gave full expressive weight to rectilinear drawing. And almost immediately he drove his pictures toward an allover evenness of accent in his so-called plus-and-minus pictures from 1914 to 1917. Then Mondrian drew back. For the results were for the most part more assertions than realizations, more statements about pictorial logic than major pictures. And given his self-imposed restriction to horizontal and vertical lines, alloverness threatened Mondrian's continued development as a painter.

To recover the possibility of variation Mondrian reverted to the traditional dominance and subordination, dramatic imbalance, or, as he called it, "dynamic equilibrium." Giving up alloverness, he retained its holistic effect. By 1920 Mondrian's surface was divided by crisp lines that exactly repeated the edges of the rectangle; all was woven together, and the picture's singleness was forced upon the viewer in a new way. Together with the extremely flat, even assertiveness of the surface, this resulted in a kind of wholeness. Rather than a balancing out of shapes within a fictive depth, one saw, as it were, the picture balancing itself out. Interestingly enough Mondrian himself regarded these pictures as paradigms of aesthetic vision.

Contrary to Mondrian, Miro and Klee exaggerated *passage* by relegating line to the foreground and shading to the background, this in an effort to free their drawing from the demands of strict rectilinearity and achieve a looser, more open feeling. In their pictures automatic graphic effects float on or in an indeterminate atmosphere evoked by softly shaded color areas, which have been tinted or stained into the surface.

Barnett Newman and Mark Rothko began with this Surrealist version of late Cubism; they eliminated the overwriting and were left with luminous and potentially penetrable and shimmering fields, which they then stiffened and flattened with simplified rectilinear design.

Olitski, too, seems to have had Miro in mind, especially around 1964. In that year he completed a series of canvases that contain only a few small dots or disks of color eccentrically positioned in a raw canvas field. These were painted at the same time as pictures like *Flaubert Red,* which show positively colored fields. And Olitski has said that what interested him most in Miro's work were the *backgrounds* of his pictures.[18] Without the overwriting, Miro's backgrounds become foreground, or rather the distinction between background and foreground is abolished. The picture becomes an allover field of light and color.

In arriving at the allover picture, Olitski had the dramatic precedent of Jackson Pollock's work. By the mid-1940's Pollock had also arrived at the Surrealist type of late Cubist picture. Starting from this point, he took a course opposite to that taken by Newman and Rothko but with similar, if more radical, results. Pollock made the *overwriting* the whole picture and in so doing rediscovered alloverness—an alloverness free of the structure of the visible world. In the best of his classical drip paintings there is a comfortable congruence between pure aesthetic regard and a surface more or less evenly articulated; between a just and even distribution of detached attention and an equalized pictorial pressure.[19]

The eye neither wanders aimlessly nor sticks at specific points, since there is a perfect harmony between the intensity of detail and the wholeness of the general aspect.

Paradoxically, Pollock's allover pictures threatened the very existence of the easel picture. As Clement Greenberg has written, "though the allover picture will, when successful, still hang dramatically on a wall, it comes very close to decoration—to the kind seen in wallpaper patterns that can be repeated indefinitely—and insofar as the all-over picture remains an easel picture, which somehow it does, it infects the notion of the genre with a fatal ambiguity."[20]

The easel picture has always depended not only on a unity perceived at a single glance but on dramatic imbalance and marked variation and hierarchies of accent. It has been Olitski's achievement to effectively reintroduce these features while retaining the essentials of the allover picture.

Both Olitski's sprayings and Pollock's drippings are relatively impersonal applications that permit the painter to achieve large scale and to work *across* the surface (rather than inward toward the center or outward from it) without any preconceived design. Both resulted in an allover, close-valued tonal field that is of more or less even tactile density yet is airy, transparent, and dissolves any sense of discrete shapes.

20
See Greenberg, "The Crisis of the Easel Picture," in *Art and Culture*, p. 55.

18
In conversation.

19
William Rubin has stressed the evenness of Pollock's allover drip pictures and related them in this regard to Impressionism. See his "Jackson Pollock and the Modern Tradition," *Artforum*, vol. 5 (February 1967), pp. 14–22; (March 1967), pp. 28–37; (April 1967), pp. 18–31; (May 1967), pp. 28–33.

On the other hand, Pollock arrived at his dripping as a way to render his line both optical and painterly.[21] But the resultant alloverness put certain limitations on his remarkably expressive drawing, the real bearer of his sensibility. Alloverness militates against highly differentiated shape development and sharp value contrasts. So it was that after 1960 Pollock, like Mondrian before him, drew back. He gave up dripping and sought to give greater accentuation and variety to his painterly draftsmanship at the expense of alloverness.[22]

Louis, in his "veils," was the first to exploit Pollock's allover, holistic field for chromatic effect. Yet staining seemed to push painting toward pure, full-intensity hues and a Fauvelike picture and in turn meant drawing, edges, and design. The solution of Noland and Louis after 1958 was to retain Pollock's holistic effect while surrendering his alloverness. Their holistic and symmetrical configurations were "noncompositional" ways to bring multiple, contrasting colors forcefully together for the viewer.

Having consigned expressive drawing to his sculpture, Olitski moved to reunite in his spray paintings the painterly and holistic allover picture with color. Spraying, by its very nature, results in a pictorial substance that is much more of a piece than Pollock's skeins and spatters. The latter are quite discrete elements, and for this reason Pollock needed to keep his articulation quite regular.

Heinrich Wölfflin noted that the linear moves toward "multiple unity," while the painterly inclines toward what he called "unified unity." The painterly is flux, "the deliverance of the forms from their isolation," while the linear separates, isolates, articulates.[23] Creating alloverness by means of the linear enforces extreme self-limitation, as can be seen in the careers of Mondrian and Pollock. The painterly yields alloverness more easily and naturally; and this is especially true of Olitski's painterliness. Appearing as one seamless paint covering, his sprayed, close-valued color fields are inherently single and cohesive. In turn this "unified unity" allows considerable articulation within itself. Unlike the brushed or dripped painterliness of Abstract Expressionism, which could not easily be equally distributed, spraying creates a smoothly continuous surface, one that easily admits color. And by placing the main burden of expression on surface texture and color, Olitski has available greater potential range and variety within the limits of alloverness than Pollock had available to him.

Abstract alloverness throws up the fact that the identification of the visual and pictorial fields can never be complete, because, among other reasons, as the pictorial field becomes relatively flat and uniform, it begins to call attention to its own distinct limits, a feature the visual field does not possess. The viewer becomes far more aware of the discreteness of the picture as an object hanging on the wall. As a consequence, the margins of the picture seem more specific, flatter, and more literal as they approach the literal edge.[24]

21
Michael Fried, *Morris Louis, 1912–1962*, Boston, Museum of Fine Arts, 1967, and William Rubin, "Jackson Pollock and the Modern Tradition."

22
A picture such as *Echo,* 1951 (Museum of Modern Art, New York), is particularly relevant in this regard, for, despite its success, one can perceive here a certain tension between Pollock's will to calligraphic variation and the demands of alloverness. Also, in this picture Pollock forgoes close values in favor of sharp opposition of black and white.

23
Heinrich Wölfflin, *Principles of Art History*, New York, Dover Publications [1956], p. 159.

24
This may be the reason why all pictures, including all flat abstract pictures, look better framed than unframed.

Pollock had often given a sense of both expansion and delimitedness to his fields and prevented this potential objecthood from invading his pictures at the sides by seeing to it that his incident slackened in the vicinity of the actual edge of the painting; that is, he rendered these areas slightly more neutral, less "painted." (In his 1958 "veils" Morris Louis did the same with still more emphasis.)

Many of Olitski's earliest spray pictures of 1965 lack interior contours or lines; as the whole surface becomes a single field, the literal edges of the rectangle start to be felt as determinate drawing,[25] a drawing that is somehow sculptural and pictorial at the same time. Again, this possibility was available to Olitski because his sprayed all-overness was much more homogeneous than Pollock's drips. Nonetheless, to insure that the proportions and edges of the picture were experienced as drawing rather than simply neutral limits, Olitski had to restrict himself to tall, narrow formats, since only these appeared to "stamp themselves out" as pictorial.[26] Also, no matter how "stamped out" and pictorial the literal edge of the rectangle becomes, it remains to a certain extent a perfectly balanced and thus slightly static shape. This is at odds with the mobile, shifting life of the interior incident. The shape of the rectangle becomes a choice sensibly distinct from the emergent logic of the field.

It was necessary to render the edge more responsive to the internal dynamics of the picture. Thus, even more important than Olitski's discovery that the literal edge of his picture could be seen as drawing was the perception that the areas near the edge provided a limited tolerance for incisive, "old-fashioned" drawing. Still in 1965, he began to introduce lines of pastel, or lines caused by maskings between spray applications, or, in 1966, strokes of impastoed paint, and, recently, lines made with a Magic Marker.

By diverting attention from the literal shape and occasionally by emphasizing it, these accents permit Olitski to employ a wider range of format shapes and sizes.[27] In the same way, they mean

25
Greenberg, "Jules Olitski," in XXXIII International Biennial Exhibition, p. 38. It should be noted that Olitski's very first spray paintings already show drawing at the edges in the form of narrow columns of darker spray marshaled at two sides. The pictures without any edge drawing occur immediately after this and into 1966. Moreover, Olitski had already introduced pastel lines along the edges of some of his 1964 stain paintings and had experimented with the idea of an internal frame as early as 1951 in the "drawing board" pictures.

26
Greenberg, "Jules Olitski."

27
The relationship between these edgings and Olitski's greater success with different formats after 1966 was first noted by Michael Fried, "Olitski and Shape," Artforum, vol. 5 (January 1967), pp. 20–21.

A word should be added here about the shapes of Olitski's pictures. From the beginning he has avoided symmetry and employed internal incident that has no visual similarity to the enclosing rectangle: rounded edges, dots, spots, or sprayed fields. This is not merely an attempt to escape cubism but an effort to so conceive the painting that its actual size and proportions are decided upon last; not a factor that is assumed but the result of the internal development of the picture. Olitski has written "Outer edge cannot be thought of as being in some ways within — it is the outmost extension of the color structure. The decision as to where the outer edge is, is final not initial" ("Painting in Color," p. 39).

Another aspect of this same procedure is the internal frame, which, like croppings at the literal edge, is a final, not an initial choice. Olitski has visually avoided squarish formats (and when he has employed them he has tended to have less success; see Greenberg, "Jules Olitski," p. 38).

Given the character of his incident, the square is too much a fixed, self-sufficient, and neutral shape; it appears a priori and not responsive enough to the interior forces of the picture.

that lateral openness, compression and release, is no longer a given, as in the first spray pictures, but now a variable subject to choice and control by the artist.[28]

Bearing no shape similarity to the field, these markings can therefore relate to it more solely in terms of color and value, while their immediate relation to the edge in terms of proximity and shape (or at least axis) means that their delimiting function is equally clear. But their specific point of occurrence along the perimeter is more than anything a compositional choice.

28
It is sometimes as if the whole picture were an enlargement of one analytical cubist plane with its disassociated shadings, highlights, and *passage*. As with the cubist plane, shading often clusters along the edges of Olitski's pictures, acting as nascent modeling. The whole surface takes on the illusion of a slightly curved relief. Or, again through shading, the plane, i.e., the field, can seem to tip or slant away from the surface (see Rosalind Krauss, "On Frontality," *Artforum,* vol. 6 [May 1968], pp. 40–46) only to be brought back again by the incisive drawing at the edges. Around 1969–70 Olitski tends to build up paint in the center so that this area becomes an opaque highlight. The whole surface seems to swell up at that point yet remains pinned down at the edges or corners.

Since Olitski's very flat, continuous, and homogeneous surfaces of very close value create sufficient organic unity, a balancing-out type of composition is superfluous; the very smoothness of this unity, however, threatens that life and drama which a value-accented composition has always given to the easel picture. Usually sharply different in value and often in texture, Olitski's marginings are eccentrically spaced and occur at one, two, or three sides and occasionally at the corners (but almost never all the way around or exactly parallel with the literal edge). As a result they throw the whole into dramatic imbalance; they render it indeterminate, less easily graspable, or they create what is called "occult balance": small, intense, differently articulated areas offsetting large, relatively empty ones. Erratic and abrupt, these edgings emphasize and are quieted by the smooth continuity and relative homogeneity of the field, to which in turn they are obviously subordinated; edge and field are no longer statically and uniformly juxtaposed as in the first spray paintings but are more actively and expressively responsive to each other. If Olitski's marks and value changes occurred at the center, they would disrupt continuity and the unity of the surface by reintroducing an illusion of depth, of foreground and background readings (as in Miro's work). Appearing at the edge, they merely lie on or near the surface, for the space cannot spread out all around—and by implication behind—a mark. Without spatial implications they merely emphasize by contrast the continuous, allover unity of the field. At the same time they render the picture, as a whole, ambiguous and dynamic.

Since 1965 Olitski has continued to insist on a close identification of pictorial looking and the pictorial surface, on wholeness and alloverness, while at the same time exploring and testing that area, at the edges, where they do not and can never coincide. He has also exploited his discovery that a sharply restricted value range and certain kinds of painterliness result in a compelling singleness of total aspect, a singleness that in turn readmits an effective degree of color and value variation. Thus, Olitski has been able to delimit his fields while reintroducing marked accentuation as well as the effect of compositional liveness, dramatic imbalance, into the allover picture, a kind of picture that by its very nature would seem to exclude these features. His style is the interface between Pollock's nonhierarchical alloverness and the dramatically articulated structures of traditional easel painting. Modernist painting since Impressionism has been art about art, and as such its history can be seen in part as a gradual rearrangement of the conventions of representation so as to make them serve purely aesthetic ends. This point had already been perceived by Mondrian, who felt that by eliminating all but horizontal and vertical lines he had isolated the basic coordinates of aesthetic seeing. And in a way perhaps he did. But modernism is both more and less than Mondrian thought. It is more historical and less universal. It depends on a continual and inspired revision of what a picture is or can be. Hence Pollock and Olitski have gone on to isolate basic facts of *pictorial seeing*. Alloverness, flatness, and an emphasis on optical color are all responses to a historical situation in which picture viewing has become the sole touchstone and impetus for picture making.

Unflinchingly accepting the most radical implications of Pollock's art, Olitski has taken on the role of finding room to extend the evolution of modernist painting, despite the seeming conclusiveness of Pollock's achievement. Not the first to arrive at the allover picture, Olitski is also not the only painter to use it as a vehicle for color. And other painters have, quite independently, hit upon the idea of introducing pronounced changes near the margins of a relatively uniform field. But no painter has grasped as clearly as Olitski the potentiality inherent in these conventions or insisted upon them with greater consistency. In his hands they have been made to yield an extraordinary range of expressive feeling. Olitski is, at least for the moment, saving the easel painting itself as a viable modernist idiom.

1

Demikov One, 1957, spackle, acrylic resin, and dry pigments on canvas, 37 x 37 in. Courtesy Lawrence Rubin Gallery, New York.

Chronology

by Elinor L. Woron

Jules Olitski, 1973

March 27, 1922

Born in Snovsk, Russia, the only child of Jevel and Anna Demi-kovsky (née Zarnitsky). His father, a commissar, is executed by the Russian government in 1921, a few months before Olitski's birth. The family subsequently moves to Gomel, Russia.*

August 1923

Emigrates with mother and grandmother to the United States. Lives in Jamaica, New York, for a few months at the home of his uncle Nathan Zarnin, whose financial assistance and sponsor-ship made their emigration possible. Moves from there to Sack-man Street, Brooklyn. Mother works to support family.

1926–1940

Mother marries Hyman Olitsky (1926), a widower with two sons, Sidney and Bernard. Half-sister Rosalyn Olitsky is born. Family remains in Brooklyn, then moves to Patchogue, Long Island, where Olitski attends elementary school. They return to Brook-lyn. He attends New York public schools: Winthrop Junior High School (1934–1937); Samuel J. Tilden High School (1937–1940). Although there is no interest in art in his family, Olitski shows particular enthusiasm and talent for drawing.

1935

Death of maternal grandmother, Frieda Zarnitsky, is a traumatic experience for Olitski, who begins to question the meaning of his own life and focus more strongly on his desire to become an artist. Occasionally attends art classes in New York City, where Chaim Gross, Moses Soyer, and Raphael Soyer are among the instructors. Olitski remembers working in plaster and wood.

1939

Sees paintings by great masters for the first time during a visit to the New York World's Fair and is particularly impressed by the Rembrandt portraits. He begins visiting museums around New York City, returning often to look at the Sargent watercolors in the Brooklyn Museum.

Wins scholarship prize to study drawing at the Pratt Institute. He remembers working tediously in charcoal for three months, perfecting the drawing of an antique portrait bust before being allowed to go on to other things.

1940

Meets Impressionist-style painter Samuel Rothbort during installation of this artist's exhibition at Tilden High School. Rothbort invites Olitski to paint with him out of doors around Sheepshead Bay. He works in oils for the first time, painting landscapes, scenes of the docks and of boats in the water.

Awarded art prize at high school graduation. Head of art department, Herbert Yates, encourages Olitski to continue his study of painting with a view toward becoming an art teacher.

*In this chronology I have made use of information provided by Jules Olitski, Dawn Andrews, Howard Conant, Michael Freilich, Sidney Geist, Clement Greenberg, Seymour Hacker, Pierre Matisse, and Kenworth Moffett, and by the following galleries: André Emmerich, David Mirvish, Poindexter, and Lawrence Rubin.

5

House of Orange, ca. 1961–1962, oil-miscible acrylic on canvas, 80 x 91⅞ in. Courtesy Lawrence Rubin Gallery, New York.

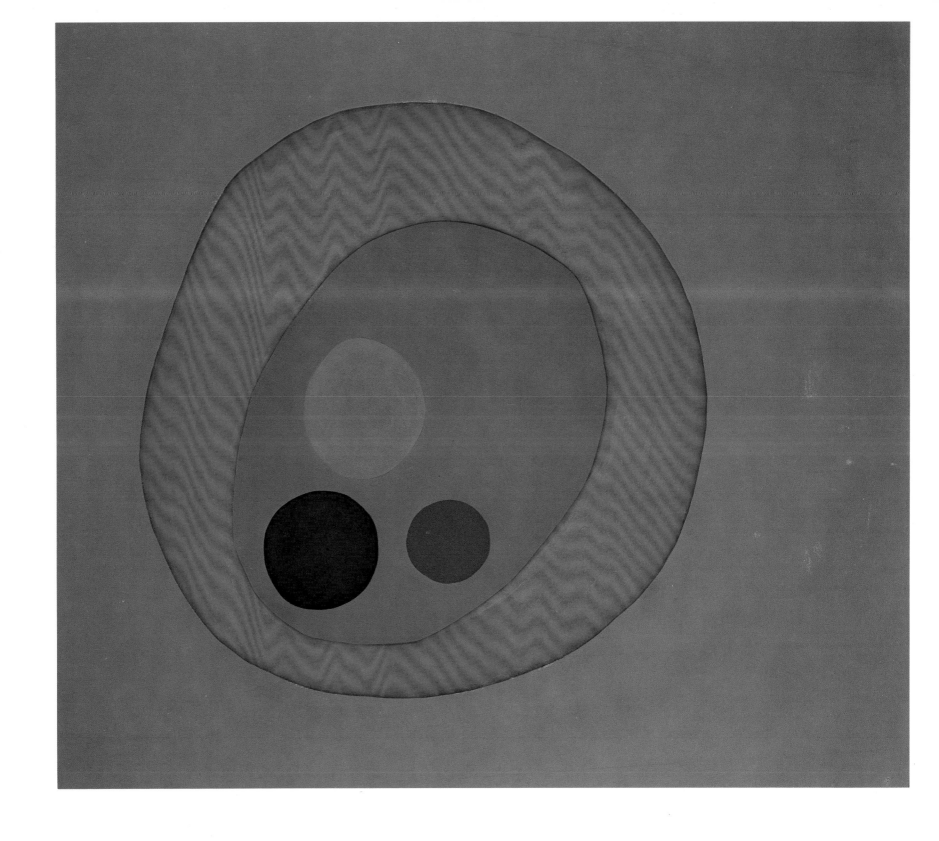

1940–1942

Admitted to the National Academy of Design, New York, where he studies life drawing and portrait painting with Sidney Dickinson, a prominent portraitist and National Academician. Studies sculpture in the evening at the Beaux Arts Institute where he works on figurative clay sculpture.

First encounter with totally abstract art is at the Museum of Non-Objective Painting (later named the Solomon R. Guggenheim Museum), then under the direction of Hilla Rebay. This experience does not influence his style at this time, however.

1942–1945

After becoming a United States citizen and legally taking his step-father's name (Olitsky), he is drafted into the United States Army. He studies at Purdue University under the auspices of the Army Specialized Training Program.

Interest in portrait painting continues. Olitski tries to imitate the style of old masters such as Rembrandt, Titian, and Velazquez by working with underpainting, glazes, scumbling, and effects of chiaroscuro. Marries Gladys Katz.

1942

Meets painter Victor Thall, who had been living in Paris and taught at the Art Student's League. A small group of young painters meet in Thall's New York apartment and submit paintings for criticism. For a time Olitski is part of this group. With Thall, he frequently visits the Museum of Modern Art and the Metropolitan Museum of Art, where he becomes interested in works of Cézanne, Manet and the Impressionists, as well as paintings by Matisse, Vlaminck, Derain, and the Nabis, Bonnard and Vuillard. Under Thall's influence he begins to use color more freely in a somewhat Fauvist manner.

1945–1948

Upon discharge from the army, Olitski lives in Brooklyn for a short time. Moves to Asheville, North Carolina, for a year where he is attracted by the local landscape. Hitchhikes with wife to Mexico, planning to spend a year painting in a fishing village, but finds the landscape and effect of sunlight too excessive and dramatic. Illness and medical expenses drain his resources, and after approximately a month, Olitski returns to New York, where he lives on Henry Street on the lower East Side of Manhattan. He moves from there to Sheepshead Bay, Brooklyn. Continues to paint Fauvelike pictures.

Studies at the Educational Alliance with Chaim Gross (1947) and becomes involved in modeling semiabstract, figurative sculptures.

Daughter Eve is born (July 1948).

1949–1951

Aided by the G.I. Bill, Olitski travels to Paris. Studies with Ossip Zadkine for a few months, then enrolls at the Académie de la Grande Chaumière, where he remains registered for a year, but does not attend classes. He has a studio outside of Paris in Chaville and later in Paris, on Rue des Suisses, near the métro Plaisance.

This is a very personal and introspective time of Olitski's life, when he questions his own identity as a painter and strains to break with his academic training. Isolates himself from his artistic surroundings, stays away from museums, including the Louvre and remains uninvolved with current European trends.

His interest in Dubuffet is aroused by Clement Greenberg's essay "School of Paris, 1946," and he goes to see Dubuffet's paintings at Galerie Rive Gauche. He also sees works by Bonnard and Braque at Galerie Maeght and paintings by Picasso and Gris at Kahnweiller's Galerie Louise Leiris.

Works on "blindfold paintings" for about six months in an attempt to break from an academic style and free himself from everything he has known and has learned to do with ease. By painting with a blindfold, then removing it to consciously reinforce forms and confirm images, he is able to overcome his own facility.

Paintings take on a somewhat synthetic Cubist look with flat areas of bright color as well as overtones of Surrealist automatic painting replete with dream, fantasy, and sexual images.

1950

Meets sculptor Sidney Geist, a member of a cooperative group of young American artists who start Galerie Huit on Rue St. Julien le Pauvre. Organized by Tajiri Shinkichi, the group also includes Oscar Chelemsky, John Anderson, Larry Calcagno, Rudolph Baranik, Reginald Pollack, and Burton Hasen. The gallery has previously been the studio of sculptor Robert Rosenwald, who was leaving Paris and offered the space to them rent free for a period of time.

Winter 1950

Participates in "Americans in Paris Exhibition" at Hacker Gallery, New York (December 5–30). Exhibition is organized by Sidney Geist and includes works by Tajiri Shinkichi, George Ortman, Gabriel Cohen, and Sidney Geist. Carlyle Burrows (*Herald Tribune,* 10 December 1950) writes that Olitski's "paintings have a savage vigor that mark the work with both intelligence and strong feeling."

1951

Olitski's first one-man show is held at Galerie Huit. He exhibits semiabstract paintings executed in bright spectral colors that developed out of the blindfold works.

Leaves Paris and returns to New York. Divorced from wife.

1952–1954

Earns B.S. degree in art education at New York University.

Works part time as assistant in Department of Art Education at New York University (1953–1956).

6

After Five, 1961, acrylic resin on canvas, 92½ x 93½ in. Collection Mr. and Mrs. David Mirvish, Toronto.

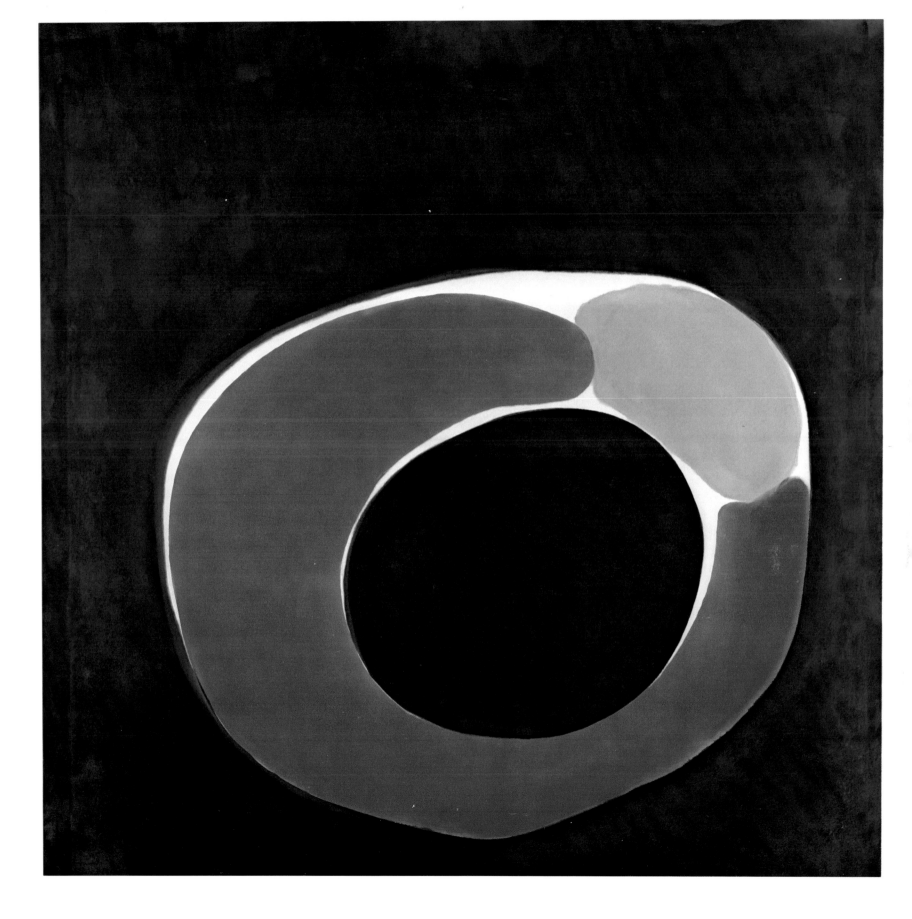

Reacts against intense, aggressive colors and imagery of Paris works. Paints monochromatic pictures using drawing boards as models, in which the center field remains empty and the painterly incident is pushed to the margins of the picture. This configuration presages Olitski's more recent work.

June 1953

First work exhibited in New York is shown at Roko Gallery in group exhibition organized by Michael Freilich. Others participating are Louise Nevelson, William King, Robert Andrew Parker, Walter Williams, and Alex Katz. Freilich describes Olitski's works of this time as landscape in feeling but moving toward a personal kind of abstraction.

1954

Occasionally exhibits work in jury-selected group shows at City Center Art Gallery.

September 1954–June 1955

Joins faculty as associate professor of art, Department of Art Education, State University College at New Paltz, New York.

1955

Earns M.A. degree at New York University. Works toward doctoral degree. Serves as curator of the New York University Art Education Gallery until 1956. Organizes exhibitions of "Contemporary Indonesian Paintings," "Paintings by Neuro-Psychiatric Patients," and "Photography," among others. Also organizes a series of panel discussions held at the gallery.

1956

Marries Andrea Hill Pearce. After living in Brooklyn for a short time, they move to East Norwich, Long Island (1958), then to Northport, Long Island. Daughter Lauren is born (March 1957).

1956–1963

Olitski is member of faculty at C.W. Post College of Long Island University, Greenvale, New York, where he becomes associate professor and chairman of the Fine Arts Department.

1958

First one-man show in the United States is an exhibition of heavily impastoed paintings at Zodiac Gallery, a small room set aside at Iolas Gallery in which works of new artists are shown. Catalogue prints Olitsky's name with the European spelling, "Olitski"; he prefers this spelling and retains it. Clement Greenberg sees the exhibition and is interested in Olitski's paintings. Greenberg becomes a close friend, whose encouragement and criticism are valued by the artist.

December 1958

Greenberg becomes consultant to French & Co. Invites Olitski to be represented by the gallery and to participate in a group show along with Friedel Dzubas, Adolph Gottlieb, Wolfgang Hollegha, Morris Louis, Barnett Newman, Kenneth Noland, and David Smith.

May 1959

One-man exhibition at French & Co. comprises impastoed paintings in which spackle, paint, colored pigments, and acrylic resins are employed. The works are executed in subtle, neutral tonalities. They suggest nonobjective bas-reliefs to Stuart Preston (*New York Times,* 24 May 1959), who feels Olitski's work occupies a territory between painting and sculpture.

Barbara Rose (*Artforum,* September 1965) writes that *Olitski's paintings* [*of this period*] *which, in their insistence on matter and texture, seem to have something to do with European "art informel" are possibly the oddest paintings done by any American of his generation. But their renunciation of space behind the frame in favor of an almost exclusively tactile involvement with a relief-like building up on top of the surface might also be seen as the acknowledgment of the contradictions in either Abstract Expressionist or "informel" painting.*

The exhibition consists of twenty-six paintings, including *Molière's Chair II* (our catalogue no. 3). During installation, Olitski meets Kenneth Noland, who helps him to hang the show.

1960

Important change in style. Begins to pour and stain dye onto larger canvases, creating sharp-edged, irregular areas of intense color on a mat black ground. Sense of texture and impasto is eliminated. Technical problems inherent in the medium, however, cause Olitski to overpaint these works with enamel. Only a few paintings of this period still exist.

April 20–May 14, 1961

Second one-man show at French & Co. comprises seventeen dye paintings. Mrs. Poindexter sees Olitski's work at this time and invites him to exhibit in her gallery.

June 1961

French & Co. closes its contemporary painting department. Olitski moves to Poindexter Gallery.

October 1961

One-man exhibition at Poindexter Gallery.

October 27, 1961–January 7, 1962

Osculum Silence (1960), a dye picture, wins second prize for painting ($1,500) at the Pittsburgh International Exhibition of Contemporary Painting and Sculpture, sponsored by the Carnegie Institute. Award jury includes Lawrence Alloway, Robert Giron, Seymour Knox, Kenzo Okada, and Daniel Cotton Rich. The exhibition comprises 524 paintings and sculptures. First prize is awarded to Mark Tobey (Untitled); third prize, Adolph Gottlieb (*Tan over Black*); fourth prize, Ellsworth Kelly (*Block Island No. 2*); fifth prize, Wolfgang Hollegha (*Bird*). *Osculum Silence* is acquired by Museum of Modern Art, New York.

8

Green Jazz, 1962, oil-miscible acrylic on canvas, 92 x 64 in. Collection J. Kasmin, London.

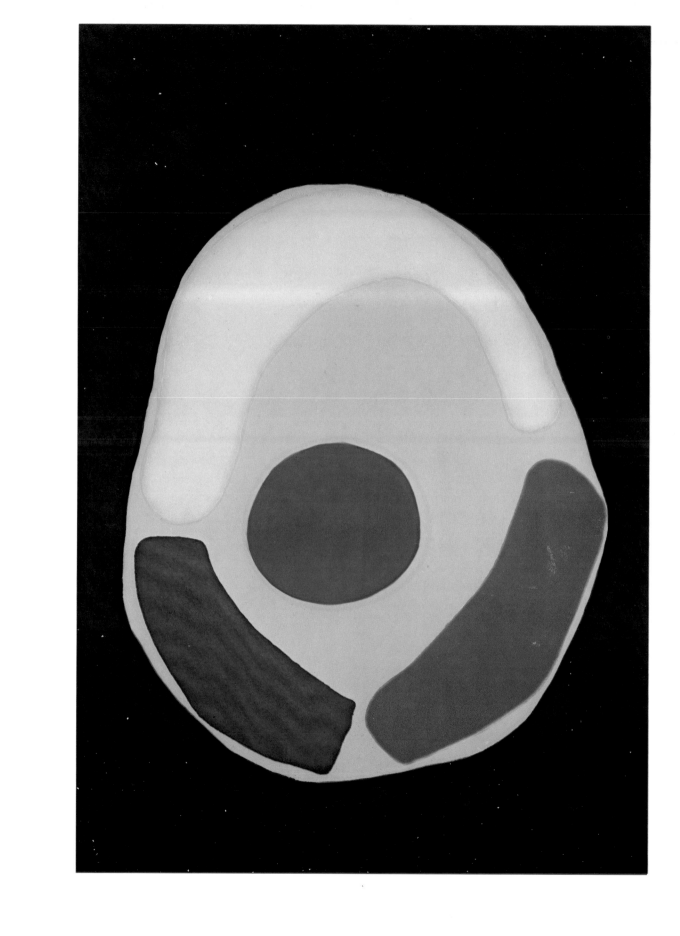

Late 1961–1962

Olitski is invited to exhibit in Italy by the dealer Toninelli. Works on a series of pictures subsequently called "Italian Paintings" because they are exhibited in Florence, Rome, and Milan. These are hard-edge works in which precisely drawn elliptical forms are executed in intense colors. Olitski begins using homemade, water-based acrylic, similar to Liquitex, applied to the canvas with brush and sponge.

Later Olitski changes to technique of staining thinned Magna acrylic into unprimed canvas with sponges, brushes, and occasionally rollers in an attempt to get away from the opacity of earlier work.

1962–1963

Paintings are organized around a central core of color or raw canvas, with alternating concentric bands of saturated color and ground expanding outward to intersect the framing edge.

Major stain painting of this period, *Born in Snovsk,* is later purchased by the Ford Foundation and presented as a gift to the Art Institute of Chicago, March 18, 1964 (our catalogue no. 9).

February 1962

One-man exhibition at Poindexter Gallery.

October–November 1962

One-man exhibition at New Gallery, Bennington College, organized by Paul Feeley, comprises six paintings: *Green Jazz, Purple Passion Company, Sacred Courtesans Blue, Pink Love, Yellow Juice, Ino Delight.*

December 11, 1962–February 2, 1963

Exhibits *Queen of Sheba Breast* in "Whitney Annual," Whitney Museum of American Art, New York.

1963

Begins to rub, stain, and roll acrylic paint into unsized canvas, often modulating one color into the next, avoiding any sense of boundary between. In these works color appears to flow downward from the top of the canvas, stopping short of the lower framing edge. *Fatal Plunge Lady* is a major painting executed in this manner (our catalogue no. 11).

Clement Greenberg ("After Abstract Expressionism," *Art International,* October 1962) remarks that the real chance taken with color in Jules Olitski's "pure" painting provokes shock among New York artists.

Barbara Rose (*Art International,* April 1963) writes
Among Jules Olitski's new works are the best paintings shown this year in New York . . . Olitski provides an infinite number of sophisticated variations, of color harmonies, of scale, of contour and of the possible relationships of parts . . . Exceeding the limits of the canvas, the forms convey an expansiveness and largeness of conception that is like the way baroque forms overflow their boundaries.

January 11–February 15, 1963

Participates in "Three New American Painters: Louis, Noland, Olitski" at the Norman Mackenzie Art Gallery, University of Saskatchewan, Regina, Canada. The exhibition is organized by Clement Greenberg, at the request of Gerald Finley, acting director of the gallery. Three paintings are included: *Green Jazz, Purple Passion Company, Ino Delight.*

In his introduction to the catalogue Greenberg states
Olitski was already exceptional when he was a portrait painter, and he remained so as the maker of thickly impastoed pictures in a European vein of abstraction, and more recently as an explorer of high-keyed combinations of very flat color. The work he showed over the last two years in New York was some of the most unconventional to be seen anywhere in American painting. Yet hardly anything he has done before matches the . . . present canvases in resolved strength or in clarity and harmony.

From this exhibition the Norman Mackenzie Art Gallery purchases *Ino Delight* (our catalogue no. 7).

February 1963

One-man exhibition at Galleria Santacroce, Florence.

March 12–30, 1963

One-man exhibition at Poindexter Gallery, New York.

April 1963

One-man exhibition at Galleria Topazia Alliata, Rome.

September 1963

Teaches at Bennington College, Bennington, Vermont, until 1967. Lives in South Shaftsbury, Vermont.

September 18–October 15, 1963

One-man exhibition at Toninelli Arte Moderne, Milan.

September 20–October 20, 1963

Exhibits *Mushroom Perfume* in "American Painting," San Francisco Museum of Art.

Winter 1963–1964

Olitski begins to use eight-inch rollers of industrial type almost exclusively to apply water-base paint, rolling one color into another so that color changes take place within the paint flow. Color fills almost entire surface. Leaves the edges bare, asserting the flatness of the picture surface and the expansive qualities of color.

January 6–February 1, 1964

One-man exhibition at Richard Gray Gallery, Chicago.

March 10–March 28, 1964

One-man show at Poindexter Gallery, New York. Eighteen paintings are included.

10

Chemise, 1963, oil-miscible acrylic on canvas, 67 x 97½ in. Courtesy Lawrence Rubin Gallery, New York.

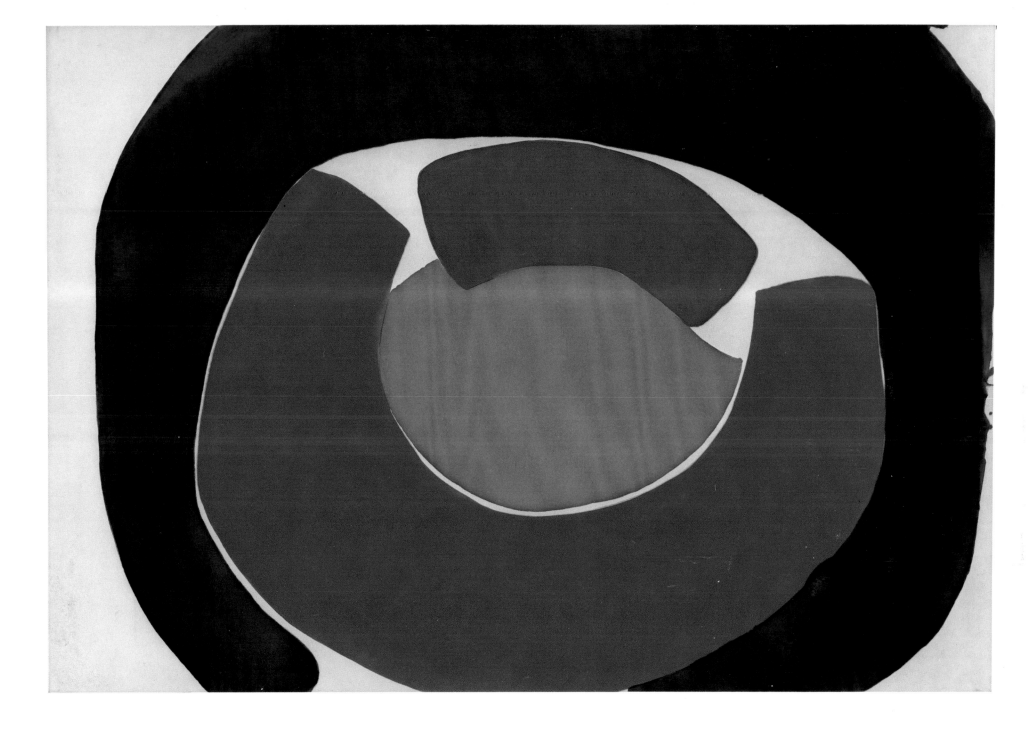

Spring 1964

Visits with Kenneth Noland at his studio in South Shaftsbury, Vermont. During a conversation with Noland and Anthony Caro, Olitski remarks that an ideal situation would be to spray color into the air and somehow have it remain there. Olitski had previously experimented with cans of spray paint on small canvases but was dissatisfied with the results. Immediately after this conversation, however, he paints his first large spray painting, using spray gun and compressor.

April 14, 1964

Museum of Modern Art, New York, exchanges *Osculum Silence* with Olitski for *Cleopatra Flesh*.

April 17, 1964

One-man exhibition at Kasmin Gallery, London.

April 23–June 7, 1964

Selected by Clement Greenberg to participate in exhibition "Post Painterly Abstraction" at Los Angeles County Museum. (Show travels to Walker Art Center, Minneapolis, and Art Gallery of Toronto.) Three paintings by Olitski are shown: *Isis Ardor, Mushroom Perfume,* and *Julius Caesar in Egypt.*
"Post Painterly Abstraction" was conceived by the Los Angeles County Museum with preceding exhibitions of Pop painting for the purpose of showing the two developments in recent American painting that had coalesced into movements. Greenberg points out in his introduction to the catalogue that most of the works in the "Post Painterly Abstraction" exhibition are a reaction against the attitudes of painterly abstraction and have in common a trend toward openness and clarity, use of high-keyed, lucid colors, anonymous execution often through the use of geometric forms and the elimination of tactile paint handling.

Summer 1964

Olitski is invited to conduct the Emma Lake Workshop, organized by the Art Department, University of Saskatchewan, Regina. Among others who have directed the workshop are Lawrence Alloway, Herman Cherry, Donald Judd, Clement Greenberg, Barnett Newman, Kenneth Noland, Frank Stella, and Michael Steiner. Olitski is the first artist to set up a studio and work there.

Works painted at this time are sometimes referred to as "curtain pictures" in which large, modulated fields of color are rolled and stained into raw canvas, spreading toward but not achieving the framing edge. These works, precursors of his spray paintings, are later exhibited in "Three American Painters," at the Fogg Museum, Cambridge.

Around this time Olitski begins to use chalk drawing on pictures as a framing device.

Fall 1964

One-man exhibition at Galerie Lawrence, Paris.

December 12, 1964–January 7, 1965

One-man exhibition of paintings executed at Emma Lake Workshop, David Mirvish Gallery, Toronto.

Spring 1965

Olitski begins to develop fully the technique of spray painting in which he draws a length of unprimed canvas through a trough of acrylic paint to saturate it. Placing wet canvas on the floor, he sprays it with pigment through spray guns, powered by an electric air compressor. Sometimes works with three guns at once, cutting back to one or two in order to create different densities of color. Later eliminates soaking process and simultaneous use of multiple guns.

Olitski works first with Magna acrylic but, because of the dangers of turpentine fumes, soon changes to water-base Aqua-tec. Also begins using a single spray gun with a variety of nozzles for greater control.

In early spray paintings the edges are free of incident. Later, perimeters are defined with brush strokes of paint, pastel, or crayon.

Rosalind Krauss discusses these paintings in her introduction to the catalogue *Jules Olitski: Recent Paintings* (Institute of Contemporary Art, University of Pennsylvania, 1968):
Jules Olitski first began to register his vision of open, undemarcated expanses of color by means of the spray technique. Even as he did so, his convictions about the role of color within the development of major abstract painting had coalesced into a deeply felt resolve . . . for Olitski, the spray medium became not only the most lucid means of expressing his own feelings about color, but a vehicle for challenging the limitations placed on color by the most radical of his contemporaries.

Michael Fried (*Artforum,* November 1965) observes
For modernism as well as neoclassicism, painting is not merely a gratification for the sight. It is a dialectical cognitive and (in the deep sense of the word) conventional enterprise which, in Jules Olitski's new paintings, has given us works to match the art of the museums in quality, conviction and—perhaps most astonishingly of all—naturalness.

March 9–April 3, 1965

One-man exhibition of paintings at Poindexter Gallery, New York.

April 21–May 30, 1965

Participates in "Three American Painters: Noland, Olitski and Stella," organized by Michael Fried at the Fogg Art Museum, Cambridge. (Exhibition circulates to Pasadena Art Museum.) The works by Olitski include paintings from Emma Lake Workshop as well as some painted earlier that summer on Stamp Act Island, Lake Wentworth, Wolfeboro, N.H.: *Deep Drag, Flaming On, Flaubert Red, Hot Ticket, Tin Lizzie Green, Strip Heresy.*

June 1965

One-man exhibition of new paintings, Kasmin Gallery, London.

11
Fatal Plunge Lady, 1963, oil-miscible acrylic on canvas, 100 x 72 in. Kasmin Ltd., London.

June 26–September 5, 1965

Participates in "Ausstellung Signale," Kunsthalle, Basel, Switzerland, where he exhibits seven paintings: *Prince Patutsky-Red, Green Jazz, Chemise, Green Love Game, Untitled, Small Black Painting, One Time Rectangle*. Also included in the exhibition are works by Al Held, Ellsworth Kelly, Hansjörg Mattmüller, Kenneth Noland, Karl Georg Pfahler, John Plumb, William Turnbull.

October 26–November 13, 1965

One-man exhibition at Poindexter Gallery, New York, shows Olitski's first spray paintings.

November 11–December 5, 1965

One-man exhibition at David Mirvish Gallery, Toronto, comprises Olitski's first spray paintings.

At this time Michael Fried writes (*Artforum*, November 1965) [*Olitski's paintings of the past nine or ten months*] *are, I believe, among the most beautiful, authoritative and moving creations of our time in any art. They differ from his own previous work in their complete freedom from anything that smacks of eccentricity, caprice or artiness; and they are distinguished from paintings in deductive formats by their ease, sensuousness and accessibility.*

Winter 1965

Begins to mask edges of already sprayed canvas around two or three sides, then sprays again and removes masking. Both a continuum of color and stenciled definition of the framing edge are achieved. He moves away from narrow vertical format to square and horizontal shaped canvas. Olitski's work begins to gain more acceptance at this time, although there is still great resistance.

June 18–October 6, 1966

Olitski is one of four painters selected by Henry Geldzahler to represent the United States in the "XXIII International Biennial Exhibition of Art," Venice, organized by the Smithsonian Institution. Other artists included are Helen Frankenthaler, Roy Lichtenstein, and Ellsworth Kelly. Olitski exhibits seven paintings: *Thigh Smoke, Lovely Scream, Of Gomel, One Eight Six, Prince Patutsky's Command, Unlocked,* and *Vertical.*

In the catalogue essay Clement Greenberg writes
Olitski has turned out what I do not hesitate to call masterpieces in every phase of his art. The masterpieces do seem to increase in frequency as color is given more rein.

June 1966

One-man exhibition at Nicholas Wilder Gallery, Los Angeles.

Autumn 1966

Olitski begins to thicken sprayed paint by adding pure ammonia to the pigment. Introduces irregular margins of impastoed paint along one, two, or three sides to define framing edge of sprayed paintings.

October 15–November 7, 1966

One-man exhibition at David Mirvish Gallery, Toronto. Comprises nine paintings of which several are executed with the thickened spray. *Doulma* (our catalogue no. 25) is among them.

October 29–November 17, 1966

One-man exhibition at André Emmerich Gallery, New York. Includes painting *Pink Alert*.

1966

Participates in exhibition "Frankenthaler, Noland, Olitski," New Brunswick Museum, St. John. (Circulates to the Norman Mackenzie Art Gallery, University of Saskatchewan, Regina; the Mendel Art Center, Saskatoon; the Confederation Art Gallery and Museum, Charlottetown, Prince Edward Island.) Five paintings included are *Zem Zem, Tea Party, Harlow Flow, Temptations, Monday Night Mark*.

Olitski moves to 44 West 96th Street, New York City, where he sets up a studio in his small apartment.

1967

Wins first prize, $2,000, and a gold medal at the "30th Biennial Exhibition of Contemporary American Painting" at the Corcoran Gallery of Art, Washington, D.C., for *Pink Alert* (our catalogue no. 28). Jury consists of three museum directors: Bartlett Hayes (Andover Gallery of American Art), Evan Turner (Philadelphia Museum of Art), and James Elliot (Wadsworth Atheneum). Other prizes go to Paul Jenkins, John McLaughlin, and Kenneth Noland. Olitski exhibits four paintings: *Pink Alert, Exact Origins, Frame Expansion,* and *Sleep Robber*. *Pink Alert* is purchased by the Friends of the Corcoran.

April–May 1967

First one-man museum show, "Olitski: Paintings 1963–1967," is held at the Corcoran Gallery of Art, Washington D.C. (Circulates to the Pasadena Art Museum and the San Francisco Museum of Art.) Exhibition comprises forty-four paintings, selected by Olitski from works completed within the previous four years. The greatest concentration is on spray paintings made since the spring of 1965, which are shown in relation to his earlier works.

The exhibition is discussed by Kermit Champa (*Art News*, May 1967):
Seeing Olitski's work of 1963–1967 together in a single exhibition, one is more aware of a continuity than of a planned or plotted development. At every point and in every picture the impact is that of pure, uninhibited color sensation. This sensation is . . . the very thing which Olitski has managed in various ways to control so that it becomes the means of expressing distinctly personal sensibilities. In the final analysis, what one has is "Olitski color" rather than just color. He has possessed it and marked it out as his own.

June 1967

Moves to 323 W. 21st Street, New York, where he sets up a studio.

14
Monkey Woman, 1964, oil-miscible acrylic on canvas, 66 x 72 in. David Mirvish Gallery, Toronto.

July 11–September 17, 1967

Exhibits *Magic Number* in "Large Scale American Paintings" at the Jewish Museum, New York.

October 21–November 9, 1967

One-man exhibition of recent paintings at André Emmerich Gallery, New York, comprises eight of his largest spray paintings shown to date.

December 9, 1967–January 5, 1968

Exhibition of sprayed paintings on paper is mounted at Poindexter Gallery, New York, in cooperation with André Emmerich Gallery, New York.

December 1967–February 1968

Exhibits *Pink Tinge* in Whitney Annual Exhibition of Contemporary American Painting, Whitney Museum of American Art, New York.

1968

Around this time begins to add gel to Aqua-tec, giving greater viscosity to the paint and a tougher, more tactile quality to the surface. Uses mops and rollers in addition to spray gun. Paints twenty-nine works in this manner, called "Esperanza," or "Hope," series.

Mixes various elements with pigments, such as varnish, metallic and pearlescent powder.

High A Yellow is acquired by the Friends of the Whitney Museum of American Art.

February 2–March 26, 1968

One-man exhibition "Jules Olitski: Recent Paintings" is organized by the Institute of Contemporary Art, University of Pennsylvania, in collaboration with the Hayden Gallery, Massachusetts Institute of Technology. Seventeen paintings are included.

April 15–May 16, 1968

One-man exhibition at David Mirvish Gallery, Toronto, comprises nine paintings. From this exhibition National Gallery of Canada purchases *DD*.

June 27–October 6, 1968

Invited to participate in "Documenta IV," Kassel, Germany. Two paintings, *Tender Boogus* (our catalogue no. 38) and *Instant Loveland,* are included.

July 10, 1968

One-man exhibition at Kasmin Gallery, London.

July–September 1968

First major attempt at sculpture. While in London, a conversation with Anthony Caro leads Olitski to make sculpture. Works in St. Neots, near Cambridge, where a large factory is available to him. Orders tubes, domes, and sheets of aluminum pretreated with an anodized color surface. He cuts, shapes, and juxtaposes the aluminum pieces in an additive process to create sculptures. Sprays them with air-drying lacquer. Completes a series of twenty sculptures within a period of seven weeks.

December 10, 1968

Shake Out is purchased by the Museum of Modern Art, New York.

February 1969

Lawrence Rubin opens gallery on 57th Street, New York. Invites Olitski to participate in his first group show. Others included are Caro, Noland, Louis, Stella, Armand, and Sandler.

April 1969

Dayton Art Institute purchases *Intimacy*.

April 1–May 18, 1969

First living American artist to be given a one-man exhibition at the Metropolitan Museum of Art, New York, entitled "The Sculptures of Jules Olitski." Henry Geldzahler selects five large constructions from the works executed at St. Neots, *Whip-out, Heartbreak of Ronald and William, Six-banger, Wheels-up,* and *Whipsaw*.

Kenworth Moffett (*The Metropolitan Museum of Art Bulletin,* April 1969) writes

Jules Olitski's first major venture into sculpture is an important event, and not simply because one of America's leading painters has turned to three dimensions. The startling originality of the works and their sheer size show that he has approached his new medium with daring; he has raised issues and opened possibilities hitherto unperceived.

June 1969

One-man exhibition of sculptures, Kasmin Gallery, London.

October 18, 1969–February 8, 1970

Selected to participate in "New York Painting and Sculpture: 1940–1970," first of the centennial exhibitions at the Metropolitan Museum of Art, New York. Olitski exhibits eight paintings, *Ten O'Clock, Bathsheba, Ritual of L, Commissar Demikovsky, Thigh Smoke, Disarmed, Green Volya, Warehouse Light,* and one sculpture, *Twelve Nights*.

November 1–December 2, 1969

One-man exhibition at Lawrence Rubin Gallery, New York, comprises eight paintings executed in acrylic emulsion on canvas.

July 1970

One-man exhibition of recent paintings at Kasmin Gallery, London.

September 15–November 1, 1970

Participates in "Color and Field, 1890–1970" at Albright-Knox Art Gallery, Buffalo. (Exhibition circulates to Dayton Art Institute.) Four paintings are included: *Commissar Demikovsky, Intimacy, Main Squeeze, 29th Hope*. *Zuloo* is subsequently purchased by Dayton Art Institute.

October 7, 1970

Albright-Knox Art Gallery, Buffalo, purchases *Second Tremor*.

15

Flaubert Red, 1964, oil-miscible acrylic on canvas, 82 x 106¾ in. Collection Rosalind Krauss, New York.

February 6–March 2, 1971

One-man exhibition of paintings executed in 1971 at David Mirvish Gallery, Toronto.

February 25–April 18, 1971

Exhibits *3rd Indomitable* (our catalogue no. 48) in "The Structure of Color" at the Whitney Museum of American Art, New York.

March 6–30, 1971

One-man exhibition at Lawrence Rubin Gallery, New York, comprises eight paintings, all acrylic emulsion on canvas.

Spring 1971

Moves to larger studio. Retains 21st Street studio until the following January.

Summer 1971

Olitski begins working in Bennington, Vermont, on a series of sculptures, which he calls "ring pieces." The constructions are of unpainted and lacquered mild steel.

January 25–March 19, 1972

Begins to use smaller and vertical format. Roughens canvas with gel, causing thickened pigment to appear more as a skin on the surface of the canvas. Uses roller or squeegee to scrape gel-thickened paint across the surface, so that variations in opacity and transparency result. Sometimes sprays color on top of this surface or brushes the edges. Colors are grayed or monotone.

April 14–May 21, 1972

Selected by Kenworth Moffett to exhibit in "Abstract Painting in the 70's: A Selection" at the Museum of Fine Arts, Boston. Four paintings, *3rd Indomitable, 8th Loosha, Orange Hook, Omsk Measure One,* are included.

April 29–May 25, 1972

One-man exhibition at Lawrence Rubin Gallery, New York, comprises eleven works, all painted in 1972.

Summer 1972

Works in Bennington, Vermont. Completes five sculptures from the "ring series," on which he has been working intermittently during the year.

June 1972

One-man exhibition of recent paintings, Kasmin Gallery, London.

The Art Institute of Chicago purchases spray painting, *Green Marfak*.

September 23–October 24, 1972

One-man exhibition of new paintings at David Mirvish Gallery, Toronto.

Winter 1972

Ken Carpenter (*Art International,* December 1972) states
The paintings of Jules Olitski seem increasingly remarkable for their tendency to elude the grasp of their audience. In part this elusiveness is due to their high quality. The best of them offer a sense of discovery that continues to emerge into consciousness long after lesser works have been fully assimilated. But even more to the point, Olitski's structure is so genuinely new that it has continually resisted perception.

January 1973

Olitski paints in preparation for exhibitions at David Mirvish Gallery, Toronto; Nicholas Wilder Gallery, Los Angeles; Lawrence Rubin Gallery, New York; and for André Emmerich's new gallery in Zurich, Switzerland. Begins to use Corten steel in new sculptures for "ring series." Museum of Modern Art, New York, acquires recent painting, *Willemites Vision*.

16

Tin Lizzy Green, 1964, oil-miscible acrylic on canvas, 115¼ x 68½ in. Courtesy Lawrence Rubin Gallery, New York.

18

Pink Shush, 1965, water-miscible acrylic on canvas, 79 x 66 in.
Private collection.

Exhibitions

Items are arranged chronologically, entered under exhibition title. Names of institutions that prepared catalogues or checklists, cities, and dates of exhibition have been included whenever information was available. Reference is made to extensive catalogue introductions or essays, and titles of exhibited works are listed.

E.L.W.

1961

The 1961 Pittsburgh International Exhibition of Contemporary Painting and Sculpture, Department of Fine Arts, Carnegie Institute, Pittsburgh, Pa., 27 October 1961–7 January 1962. Catalogue, with introduction by Gordon Bailey Washburn. (One painting: *Osculum Silence.*)

1962

Recent Acquisitions, Museum of Modern Art, New York, 20 November 1962–3 January 1963. Checklist. (One painting: *Cleopatra Flesh.*)

Whitney Annual Exhibition of Contemporary American Painting, Whitney Museum of American Art, New York, 11 December 1962–2 February 1963. Catalogue. (One painting: *Queen of Sheba Breast.*)

1963

Three New American Painters: Louis, Noland, Olitski, Norman Mackenzie Art Gallery, University of Saskatchewan, Regina, Canada, 11 January–15 February. Catalogue, with introduction by Clement Greenberg. (Three paintings: *Green Jazz, Purple Passion Company, Ino Delight.*)

Aspects of 20th Century Painting, Worcester Art Museum, Worcester, Mass., 7 February–7 April. Checklist. (One painting: *Cadmium Orange of Dr. Frankenstein.*)

The Formalists, The Washington Gallery of Modern Art, Washington, D.C., 6 June–7 July. Catalogue. (Two paintings: *Isis Ardor, Yaksi Juice.*)

Directions: American Painting, San Francisco Museum of Art, San Francisco, 20 September–20 October. Checklist. (One painting: *Mushroom Perfume.*)

New Directions in American Painting, Organized by the Rose Art Museum, Brandeis University, Waltham, Mass. Exhibited at Munson-Williams-Proctor Institute, Utica, New York, 1 December 1963–5 January 1964; Isaac Delgado Museum of Art, New Orleans, La., 7 February–8 March 1964; Atlanta Art Association, Atlanta, Ga., 18 March–22 April 1964; J. B. Speed Art Museum, Louisville, Ky., 4 May–7 June 1964; Art Museum, Indiana University, Bloomington, Ind., 22 June–20 September 1964; Washington University, St. Louis, 5–30 October 1964; Detroit Institute of Arts, 10 November–6 December 1964. Catalogue, with introduction by Sam Hunter. (One painting: *Yaksi Juice.*)

19

Bat, 1965, water-miscible acrylic on canvas, 108 x 72 in. Kasmin Ltd., London.

1964

67th Annual American Exhibition, The Art Institute of Chicago, Chicago, Ill., 28 February–12 April. Catalogue. (Two paintings: *Equator Crossing, Born in Snovsk.*)

The Atmosphere of 1964, Institute of Contemporary Art, University of Pennsylvania, Philadelphia, 17 April–1 June. Checklist. (Four paintings: *Butterfly Kiss, Doozhie Orgy, Flaming Passion of Beverly Torrid, Beautiful Bald Woman.*)

Post Painterly Abstraction, Los Angeles County Museum of Art, Los Angeles, 23 April–7 June; Walker Art Center, Minneapolis, Minn., 13 July–16 August; Art Gallery of Toronto, Toronto, 20 November–20 December. Catalogue, with introduction by Clement Greenberg. (Three paintings: *Isis Ardor, Mushroom Perfume, Julius Caesar in Egypt.*)

American Drawings, 1964, The Solomon Guggenheim Museum, New York, 17 September–27 October. Catalogue, with introduction by Lawrence Alloway. (Four pastels on paper, all untitled.)

1965

Three American Painters (Noland, Olitski and Stella), Fogg Art Museum, Harvard University, Cambridge, Mass., 21 April–30 May; Pasadena Art Museum, Pasadena, 6 July–3 August. Catalogue, with introduction by Michael Fried. (Six paintings: *Deep Drag, Flaming On, Flaubert Red, Hot Ticket, Tin Lizzie Green, Strip Heresy.*)

Ausstellung Signale, Kunsthalle, Basel, Switzerland, 26 June–5 September. Catalogue. (Seven paintings: *Prince Patutsky Red, Green Jazz, Chemise, Green Love Game, Untitled, Small Black Painting, One Time Rectangle.*)

1966

Frankenthaler, Noland, Olitski, New Brunswick Museum, St. John; The Norman Mackenzie Art Gallery, University of Saskatchewan, Regina; The Mendel Art Center, Saskatoon; The Confederation Art Gallery and Museum, Charlottetown, Prince Edward Island, Canada. Catalogue, with introduction by Barry J. Lord. (Five paintings: *Zem Zem, Tea Party, Harlow Flow, Temptations, Monday Night Mark.*)

XXXIII International Biennial Exhibition of Art, United States Pavillion, Venice, 18 June–16 October. Introduction by Henry Geldzahler, essay by Clement Greenberg. Remarks by the artist. (Seven paintings: *Lovely Scream, Of Gomel, One Eight Six, Prince Patutsky's Command, Thigh Smoke, Unlocked, Vertical.*)

1967

30th Biennial Exhibition of Contemporary American Painting, The Corcoran Gallery of Art, Washington, D.C. (Award: Corcoran Gold Medal and William A. C. Clark Prize), 24 February–19 April. Catalogue. (Four paintings: *Exact Origin, Frame Expansion, Pink Alert, Sleep Robber.*)

Form, Color, Image, Detroit Institute of Arts, Detroit, 11 April–21 May. Catalogue, with introduction by Gene Baro. (Three paintings: *Deep Suze, Summer, Thigh Smoke.*)

Ninth Tokyo Biennale, Tokyo, Japan, May. Catalogue. (One painting: *Galliloo.*)

A Selection of Paintings and Sculptures from the Collections of Mr. and Mrs. Robert Rowan, University of California, Irvine, 2–21 May; San Francisco Museum of Art, San Francisco, 2 June–2 July. Checklist. (Eight paintings: *Julius Orange, Prince Patutsky in Bennington, Arnolfini Baby, Deep Drag, Flaming On, Purple Casanova, Beatrice Blue, Juice.*)

Focus on Light, The New Jersey State Museum, Trenton, 20 May–10 September. Catalogue with introduction by Lucy R. Lippard. (One painting: *Prinkep.*)

Large-Scale American Paintings, The Jewish Museum, New York, 11 July–17 September. Checklist. (One painting: *Magic Number.*)

Torcuato di Tella International Prize Exhibition, Instituto Torcuato di Tella, Buenos Aires, Argentina; 29 September–29 October. Catalogue. (One painting: *Thigh Smoke.*)

Art for Embassies, organized by the Washington Gallery of Modern Art, 30 September–5 November. Catalogue, with introduction by Henry Geldzahler. (One painting: *Turkey Girl.*)

Jules Olitski: Paintings, 1963–1967, The Corcoran Gallery of Art, Washington, D.C., 28 April–11 June; The Pasadena Art Museum, Pasadena, 1 August–10 September; San Francisco Museum of Art, San Francisco, 26 September–5 November. Catalogue, with introduction by Michael Fried. (Forty-four paintings.)

Whitney Annual Exhibition of Contemporary American Painting, Whitney Museum of American Art, New York, 13 December 1967–4 February 1968. Catalogue. (One painting: *Pink Tinge.*)

1968

Jules Olitski; Recent Paintings, Institute of Contemporary Art, University of Pennsylvania, Philadelphia, 21 February–26 March, in collaboration with the Hayden Gallery, Massachusetts Institute of Technology, 29 March–23 April. Catalogue, with introduction by Rosalind Krauss. (Seventeen paintings.)

Documenta IV, Kassel, Germany, 27 June–6 October. Catalogue, with essay by Jean Leering. (Two paintings: *Tender Boogus, Instant Loveland.*)

Signals in the '60's, Honolulu Academy of Arts, Honolulu, Hawaii, 5 October–10 November. Catalogue, with introduction by James John Sweeney. (One painting: *C+J&B.*)

L'Art Vivant, 1965–1968, Fondation Maeght, St. Paul-de-Vence, France, 13 April–30 June. Catalogue, with introduction by François Wehrlin. (One painting: *Vabo.*)

Albert Pilavin Collection: Twentieth Century American Art, 7 October–23 November. Catalogue. *(Bulletin of the Rhode Island School of Design.)* (One painting: *Sensay.*)

21
Comprehensive Dream, 1965, water-miscible acrylic on canvas, 113 x 93 in. Collection Mr. and Mrs. Robert Rowan, Pasadena.

1969

Selections from the Richard Brown Baker Collection, Art Gallery, University of Notre Dame, Ind., 5 January–23 February. Catalogue. (One painting: *Queen of Sheba Breast.*)

The Development of Modernist Painting: Jackson Pollock to the Present, Steinberg Art Gallery, Washington University Gallery of Art, St. Louis, 1–30 April. Catalogue, with introduction by Robert T. Buck, Jr. (One painting: *Free and Fast.*)

The Sculpture of Jules Olitski, The Metropolitan Museum of Art, New York, 10 April–18 May. Essay by Kenworth Moffett, *Metropolitan Museum of Art Bulletin,* vol. 27, April 1969. (Five sculptures: *Whip-out, Heartbreak of Ronald and William, Six-banger, Wheels-up,* and *Whipsaw.*)

Concept, Vassar College Art Gallery, Poughkeepsie, N.Y., 30 April–1 June. Catalogue, with "Some Observations on Concept" by Mary Delahoyd. (One painting: *Gearing Up.*)

The Gosman Collection, Art Gallery of the University of Pittsburgh, Department of Fine Arts, 14 September–10 October. Catalogue, with essay by Aaron Sheon. (One painting: *Inside Voyage.*)

American Art of the 60's: Toronto Private Collections, York University, Toronto, Canada, 1969. Catalogue, with foreword by Michael Greenwood. (Two paintings: *Harlow Flow, Fourth Caliph.*)

Contemporary American Painting and Sculpture from the Collection of Mr. and Mrs. Eugene Schwartz, Everson Museum, Syracuse, N.Y., 13 July–16 November; University Art Gallery, State University of New York at Albany, 3 December 1969– 25 January 1970. Catalogue. (Two paintings: *Strip Heresy, Shake Up.*)

New York Painting and Sculpture: 1940–1970, The Metropolitan Museum of Art, New York, 18 October 1969–8 February 1970. Catalogue, with introduction by Henry Geldzahler. (Eight paintings: *Ten O'Clock, Bathsheba, Ritual of L, Commissar Demikovsky, Thigh Smoke, Disarmed, Green Valya, Warehouse Lights;* one sculpture: *Twelve Nights.*)

Painting in New York: 1944–1969, Pasadena Art Museum, Pasadena, 24 November 1969–11 January 1970. Catalogue, with "Some Observations about New York Painting" by Alan Solomon. (Three paintings: *Flaming On, Susie Wiles, Prince Patutsky in Bennington.*)

1969 Annual Exhibition of Contemporary American Painting, Whitney Museum of American Art, New York, 16 December 1969–1 February 1970. Catalogue. (One painting: *Embrace.*)

1970

69th Annual American Exhibition, Art Institute of Chicago, Chicago, 17 January–22 February. Catalogue. (Two paintings: *Outrider, Goozler.*)

American Artists of the Nineteen-Sixties. Centennial Exhibition, Boston University, School of Fine and Applied Arts, Boston, 6 February–14 March. Catalogue, with essay by H. Harvard Arnason. (One painting: *Main Squeeze.*)

Color, UCLA Art Galleries, 15 February–22 March. Catalogue, with essay on Jules Olitski by Lynn Bailess and Carol Donnell. (Four paintings: *Optimum, Surface Scrambler, Untitled, EE;* one sculpture: *Bunga.*)

Contemporary Painting and Sculpture, Wellesley College Museum, Jewett Art Center, Wellesley, Mass., 7 March–26 April. Catalogue. (Three paintings: *Beyond Bounds, Paid Model, Green Hands;* one sculpture: *Whipsaw.*)

Giant Images of Today, Everson Museum of Art, Syracuse, N.Y., 15 August–30 September. Catalogue. (One painting: *Disarmed.*)

35th Annual Exhibition, Butler Institute of American Art, Youngstown, Ohio, 28 June–30 August. (One painting: *Masker.*)

Two Generations of Color Painting, Institute of Contemporary Art, University of Pennsylvania, Philadelphia, 1 October– 6 November. Catalogue, with introduction by Stephen S. Prokopoff. (One painting: *Green Marfak.*)

Selections from the Mr. and Mrs. Robert A. Rowan Collection, Pasadena Art Museum, Pasadena, 15 November 1970. Check-list. (Six paintings: *Juice, Comprehensive Dream, Deep Drag, Arnolfini Baby, Drakely, Tender Boogus.*)

Painting and Sculpture Today. Contemporary Art Society and Indianapolis Museum of Art, Indianapolis. Catalogue, with introduction by Richard L. Warrum. (One painting: *Secret Pearlessence.*)

Color and Field: 1890–1970, Albright-Knox Art Gallery, Buffalo, New York, 15 September–1 November; The Dayton Art Institute, 20 November 1970–10 January 1971; The Cleveland Museum of Art, 4 February 1971–28 March 1971. Catalogue, with introduction by Priscilla Colt. (Four paintings: *Commissar Demikovsky, Intimacy, Main Squeeze, 29th Hope.*)

The Drawing Society National Exhibition, 1970, circulating exhibition 1970–72. Catalogue, with introduction by James Biddle. "Thoughts on Drawing" by Robert Motherwell. (One pencil drawing: *Nude III.*)

25

Doulma, 1966, water-miscible acrylic on canvas, 68½ x 90 in. Collection Mr. and Mrs. David Mirvish, Toronto.

1971

Contemporary American Painting and Sculpture: Selections from the Collection of Mr. and Mrs. Eugene M. Schwartz, Milwaukee Art Center, 22 January–28 February. Catalogue, with introduction by Carl Schmalz. (Three paintings: *Shake Up, Strip Heresy, Short.*)

The Structure of Color, Whitney Museum of American Art, New York, 25 February–18 April. Catalogue, with essay by Marcia Tucker; statement by the artist. (One painting: *3rd Indomitable.*)

Jules Olitski, University of Michigan Museum of Art, 11 April– 9 May. Checklist, with statement by the artist. "Painting in Color," reprinted from *Artform* (January 1967). (Seven paintings: *10th Loosha, 3rd Loosha, 2nd Indomitable, Front Breaker #2, Goozler, Female Shiver, EE.*)

The Deluxe Show, sponsored by the Ménil Foundation, Houston, Texas, 15 August–12 September. Catalogue, with introduction by Steve Cannon; interview with Clement Greenberg by Simone Swan. (One painting: *Loosha One.*)

The Vincent Melzac Collection, The Corcoran Gallery of Art, Washington, D.C., 1971. Catalogue, with introduction by Ellen Gross Landau; retrospective notes on the Washington School by Barbara Rose. (One painting: *Cadmium Orange of Dr. Frankenstein.*)

1972

Whitney Annual Exhibition of Contemporary American Painting, Whitney Museum of American Art, New York, 25 January–19 March. Catalogue. (One painting: *Irkutsk Dawn.*)

Color Painting, Amherst College, Amherst, 4 February–3 March. (One painting: *Irkutsk.*)

Abstract Painting in the 70's: A Selection, Museum of Fine Arts, Boston, 14 April–21 May. Catalogue, with introduction by Kenworth Moffett. (Four paintings: *3rd Indomitable, 8th Loosha, Orange Hook, Omsk Measure.*)

Masters of the Sixties, Edmonton Art Gallery, Edmonton, Alberta, Canada, 4 May–4 June. Catalogue, with introduction by Karen Wilkin. (One painting: *Goozler;* one sculpture: *St. Neots Night.*)

Twentieth Century Prints from the Dartmouth College Collection, compiled by members of the History of Prints Seminar, Department of Art, Hanover, N.H., 19 May–9 July. (One silkscreen: *Untitled, 1970.*)

Contemporary Art: The Collection of Dr. and Mrs. Joseph Gosman, University of Michigan Museum of Art, 13 September– 15 October. Catalogue. (One painting: *Inside Voyage.*)

36

End Run, 1967, water-miscible acrylic on canvas, 81 x 48 in. Courtesy Lawrence Rubin Gallery, New York.

Lavender Liner, 1967, water-miscible acrylic on canvas, 65 x 180 in. Collection Kenneth Noland, New York.

Bibliography

Items are arranged in chronological sequence according to year of publication and listed alphabetically by author within each year. Included are selected catalogues with extensive essays, journal and newspaper articles, and reviews.

E.L.W.

1959

Campbell, Lawrence. "Jules Olitski." *Art News*, vol. 58 (May 1959), p. 50.

Preston, Stuart. "Three Generations of Moderns." *New York Times*, 24 May 1959, p. 17.

Tillim, Sidney. "Jules Olitski." *Arts Magazine*, vol. 33 (June 1959), p. 56.

1961

Canaday, John. "International Exhibition Opens in Pittsburgh." *New York Times*, 27 October 1961, p. 66.

1963

Greenberg, Clement. Introduction to *Three New American Painters: Louis, Noland, Olitski*. [Catalogue.] Regina, Canada, Norman Mackenzie Art Gallery. (Reprinted in *Canadian Art*, vol. 20 [May 1963], pp. 172–175.)

Hudson, Andrew. "Art." *The Nor'wester*, Saskatoon, 17 January 1963.
—. "On looking at the New Paintings." *Regina Saskatoon Review*, 5 August 1963.

Rose, Barbara. "New York Letter." *Art International*, vol. 7 (April 1963), pp. 57–58.

1964

Fried, Michael. "New York Letter." *Art International*, vol. 8 (May 1964), pp. 40–42.

Greenberg, Clement. Introduction to *Post Painterly Abstraction*. [Catalogue.] Los Angeles County Museum of Art. (Reprinted in *Art International*, vol. 8 [Summer 1964], pp. 63–65.)

1965

Fried, Michael. "Jules Olitski's New Paintings." *Artforum*, vol. 4 (November 1965), pp. 36–40.
—. Introduction to *Three American Painters: Noland, Olitski, and Stella*. [Catalogue.] Cambridge, Mass., Fogg Art Museum.

Hudson, Andrew. "Viewpoint on Art." *Washington Post*, 31 October 1965, p. G-7.

Kozloff, Max. "Frankenthaler and Olitski." *The Nation*, vol. 200 (April 1965), pp. 374–376.

Lippard, Lucy. "New York Letter." *Art International*, vol. 9 (May 1965), p. 55.

Lynton, Norbert. "London Letter." *Art International*, vol. 9 (September 1965), p. 50.

Rose, Barbara. "The Second Generation: Academy and Breakthrough." *Artforum*, vol. 4 (September 1965), pp. 53–62.

39
Doessy, 1967, water-miscible acrylic on canvas, 51¾ x 19¾ in. Courtesy Lawrence Rubin Gallery, New York.

1966

Fried, Michael. "Shape as Form: Frank Stella's New Paintings." *Artforum*, vol. 5 (November 1966), pp. 18–27.

Geldzahler, Henry. "Frankenthaler, Kelly, Lichtenstein, Olitski: A Preview of the American Selection at the 1966 Venice Biennale." *Artforum*, vol. 5 (June 1966), pp. 32–38.

Greenberg, Clement. "Jules Olitski." In *XXXIII International Biennial Exhibition of Art*. Venice, 1966.

Hudson, Andrew. "New York Shows Reveal Artists on the Rise—and in Decline." *Washington Post*, 6 November 1966, p. G-9.
—. "Biennial Begins Season—At Last." *Washington Post*, 4 December 1966, p. G-1.
—. "Viewpoint on Art." *Washington Post*, 25 December 1966, p. G-9.

Kramer, Hilton. "Art: (Jules Olitski)." *New York Times*, 5 November 1966, p. 26.

Lippard, Lucy. "New York Letter." *Art International*, vol. 10 (January 1966), pp. 90–91.

Lord, Barry J. Introduction to *Frankenthaler, Noland, Olitski*. [Catalogue.] St. John, New Brunswick Museum.

—. "Three American Painters Tour Canada." *Canadian Art*, vol. 23 (July 1966), p. 50.

Meadmore, Clement. "New York Scene II: Color as an Idiom." *Art and Australia*, vol. 3 (March 1966), pp. 288–291.

Mellow, James R. "New York Letter." *Art International*, vol. 10 (December 1966), pp. 61–64.

Millen, Ronald. "Fun and Games in Venice." *Art and Australia*, vol. 4 (November 1966), pp. 63–64.

Noland, Cornelia. "The 1966 Venice Biennale." *The Washingtonian*, vol. 2 (November 1966), p. 41.

Olitski, Jules. "Painting in Color." In *XXXIII International Biennial Exhibition of Art*. Venice, 1966.

Scott, David. "America's Role in the Biennale." *The Art Gallery*, vol. 9 (June 1966), p. 10.

Solomon, Alan. "American Art between Two Biennales." *Metro II*, Spring 1966.
—. "The Green Mountain Boys." *Vogue*, vol. 148 (August 1966), pp. 104–109, 151–152.

Volpi, Marisa. "Qui U.S.A.: Biennale in Anteprima." *La Fiera Letteraria*, June 1966.

1967

Baro, Gene. "Washington and Detroit." *Studio International*, vol. 174 (July–August 1967), pp. 49–51.
—. Introduction to *Form, Color, Image*. [Catalogue.] Detroit Institute of Arts.

Champa, Kermit S. "Olitski: Nothing but Color." *Art News*, vol. 66 (May 1967), pp. 36–38, 74–76.
—. "Albert Stadler: New Paintings." *Artforum*, vol. 5 (September 1967), pp. 30–34.

Feldman, Anita. "In the Museums: Large Scale American Paintings." *Arts Magazine*, vol. 42 (September–October 1967), p. 52.
—. "In the Galleries." *Arts Magazine*, vol. 42 (December 1967–January 1968), p. 58.

Fried, Michael. "Olitski and Shape." *Artforum*, vol. 5 (January 1967), pp. 20–21.
—. Introduction to *Jules Olitski, Paintings 1963–1967*. [Catalogue.] Washington, D.C., Corcoran Gallery of Art.
—. "Ronald Davis: Surface and Illusion." *Artform*, vol. 5 (April 1967), pp. 37–41.
—. "Art and Objecthood." *Artforum*, vol. 5 (Summer 1967), pp. 12–23.

Hudson, Andrew. "Biennial is a Four Star Show." *Washington Post*, 5 March 1967, p. F-8.
—. "A Painter Breaks New Ground." *Washington Post*, 9 April 1967, p. H-8.
—. "Washington: An 'American Salon' of 1967." *Art International*, vol. 9 (April 1967), pp. 73–79.
—. "Shows are Rich in Comparison." *Washington Post*, 21 May 1967, p. H-8.
—. "The 1967 Pittsburgh International." *Art International*, vol. 11 (Christmas 1967), pp. 57–64.

Kozloff, Max. "New York," *Artforum*, vol. 6 (December 1967), p. 52.

Kramer, Hilton. "Art: Corcoran Prizes No Surprises." *The New York Times*, 24 February 1967, p. 32.

Lippard, Lucy R. Introduction to *Focus on Light*. [Catalogue.] Trenton, New Jersey State Museum.

McQuillan, Melissa. "New York Reviews." *Harvard Art Review*, vol. 2 (Winter 1967). pp. 49–50.

Mellow, James R. "New York Letter." *Art International*, vol. 11 (Christmas 1967), pp. 72–73.

Olitski, Jules. "Painting in Color." *Artforum*, vol. 5 (January 1967), p. 20 (slightly revised and expanded version of Olitski's statement in *XXXIII International Biennial Exhibition of Art*, Venice, June 1966).

Pincus-Witten, Robert. "New York." *Artforum*, vol. 6 (December 1967), pp. 52–53.

Rose, Barbara. "Abstract Illusionism." *Artforum*, vol. 6 (October 1967), pp. 33–37.
—. "Washington Scene." *Artforum*, vol. 6 (November 1967), pp. 56–57.

Rosenberg, Harold. "The Art World." *The New Yorker*, vol. 43 (26 August 1967), pp. 90, 93–97.

Tillim, Sidney. "Scale and the Future of Modernism." *Artforum*, vol. 6 (October 1967), pp. 14–18.

Von Meier, Kurt. "Los Angeles." *Art International*, vol. 11 (October 1967), pp. 57–59.

41

Green Pressure, 1968, water-miscible acrylic on canvas, 118½ x 53½ in. Collection Kenneth Noland, New York.

1968

Burton, Scott. "Reviews and Previews: Jules Olitski at Poindexter Gallery." *Art News,* vol. 66 (February 1968), p. 15.

Daneili, Fidel. "Jules Olitski." *Art Digest Newsletter,* vol. 3 (1 November 1968), p. 5.

Donohoe, Victoria. "King-size Paintings Surging with Color." *The Philadelphia Inquirer,* 25 February 1968.

Driscoll, Edgar, Jr. "Artist Romero Opens New Gallery." *The Boston Globe,* (2 April 1968), p. 20.

Glueck, Grace. "Alone at Last—with a Trend." *New York Times,* 1 December 1968, p. 41.

Gouk, Alan. "Apropos of Some Recent Exhibitions in London." *Studio International,* vol. 176 (October 1968), pp. 125–126.

Grafly, Dorothy. "Diverse Styles Reflect the Vast and the Intimate." *Philadelphia Bulletin,* 25 February 1968.

Harrison, Charles. "London Commentaries: Jules Olitski at the Kasmin Gallery." *Studio International,* vol. 176 (September 1968), pp. 86–87.

Hudson, Andrew. "On Jules Olitski's Paintings and Some Changes of View." *Art International,* vol. 12 (January 1968), pp. 31–36.

Krauss, Rosalind E. Introduction to *Jules Olitski: Recent Paintings.* [Catalogue.] Philadelphia, Institute of Contemporary Art, University of Pennsylvania.

—. "On Frontality." *Artforum,* vol. 6 (May 1968), pp. 40–46.

Kudielka, Robert. "Documenta 4: A Critical Review." *Studio International,* vol. 176 (September 1968), p. 78.

Leering, Jean. "Post Painterly Abstraction," in *Documenta IV.* Kassel, Germany.

Nemser, Cindy. "In the Galleries: Jules Olitski." *Arts Magazine,* vol. 43 (December 1968–January 1969), p. 63.

"Olitski Show Opens U. of P. Arts Building." *Sunday Bulletin* (Philadelphia), 18 February 1968.

Perreault, John. "Art: Jules Olitski." *The Village Voice,* 28 November 1968, p. 19.

Sweeney, James J. Introduction to *Signals in the '60's.* [Catalogue.] Honolulu Academy of Arts, Honolulu.

Tillim, Sidney. "Evaluations and Re-evaluations: A Season's End Miscellany." *Artforum,* vol. 6 (Summer 1968), pp. 20–23.

1969

Ashton, Dore. "Esempi recenti di pittura non oggttiva negli Stati Uniti." *L'Arte moderna,* vol. 13, pp. 94, 114.

—. "New York Commentary." *Studio International,* vol. 178 (July–August 1969), p. 28.

Buck, Robert T., Jr. Introduction to *The Development of Modernist Painting: Jackson Pollock to the Present.* [Catalogue.] St. Louis, Steinberg Gallery of Art, Washington University.

Campbell, Lawrence. "Reviews and Previews." *Art News,* vol. 68 (December 1969), p. 69.

Canaday, John. "Pleased Here, Puzzled There." *New York Times,* 25 December 1969, p. 25.

Chisholm, Shirley. "Jules Olitski." In *Current Biography,* vol. 30, no. 9 (October 1969), pp. 31–34.

Delahoyd, Mary. "Some Observations on Concept." In *Concept,* Poughkeepsie, N.Y., Vassar College Art Gallery.

Feldman, Anita. "In the Galleries." *Arts Magazine,* vol. 44 (December 1969–January 1970), p. 68.

Greenwood, Michael. Introduction to *American Art of the Sixties in Toronto: Private Collections.* [Catalogue.] Toronto, York University.

Kramer, Hilton. "Sculpture: The Debut of Jules Olitski." *New York Times,* 12 April 1969, p. 31.

Kurtz, Stephen A. "Reviews and Previews: Jules Olitski." *Art News,* vol. 68 (January 1969), p. 25.

Mellow, James R. "New York Letter." *Art International,* vol. 13 (Summer 1969), p. 51.

Moffett, Kenworth. "The Sculpture of Jules Olitski." *The Metropolitan Museum of Art Bulletin,* vol. 27, no. 8 (April 1969), pp. 366–371. (Revised and reprinted in *Artforum,* vol. 7 [April 1969], pp. 55–59.)

Olitski, Jules. "On Sculpture." *The Metropolitan Museum of Art Bulletin,* vol. 27 (April 1969). p. 366. (Reprinted in *Art Now: New York,* vol. 1 [May 1969], n. p.)

Platt, Susan. "Notes on the Albert Pilavin Collection: Twentieth-Century American Art." *Bulletin of the Rhode Island School of Design,* Summer 1969, pp. 37–39.

Schjeldahl, Peter. "New York Letter." *Art International,* vol. 13, (Summer 1969), p. 64.

Sheon, Aaron. Introduction to *The Gosman Collection.* [Catalogue.] Pittsburgh, Art Gallery of the University of Pittsburgh, Department of Fine Arts.

Shirey, David L. "New York Painting and Sculpture 1940-1970." *Arts Magazine,* vol. 44 (September–October 1969), p. 35.

Solomon, Alan. "Some Observations about New York Painting." *Painting in New York: 1944–1969,* Pasadena Art Museum.

44

13th Hope, 1969, water-miscible acrylic on canvas, 60 x 22 in. Courtesy Lawrence Rubin Gallery, New York.

1970

Bailess, Lynn, and Donnell, Carol. "Jules Olitski." In *Color*. Los Angeles: U.C.L.A. Art Council, 1970, pp. 36–40.

Colt, Priscilla. "Some Recent Acquisitions of Contemporary Painting." *The Dayton Art Institute Bulletin*, vol. 28 (March 1970), p. 11.

—. Introduction to *Color and Field: 1890–1970*. [Catalogue.] Buffalo, Albright-Knox Art Gallery.

Fenton, Terry. "In the Galleries—Toronto: The David Mirvish Opening Show." *Arts Canada*, vol. 27 (December 1970), pp. 57–58.

Geldzahler, Henry. Introduction to *New York Painting and Sculpture: 1940–1970*. [Catalogue.] New York, The Metropolitan Museum of Art, 1970.

Gouk, Alan. "An Essay on Painting." *Studio International*, vol. 180 (October 1970), pp. 145–148.

Hilton, Timothy. "Commentary." *Studio International*, vol. 180 (September 1970), p. 100.

Prokopoff, Stephen S. Introduction to *Two Generations of Color Painting*. [Catalogue.] Philadelphia, Institute of Contemporary Art, University of Pennsylvania, 1970.

Rose, Barbara. "The Spiritual in Art." *Vogue Magazine*, vol. 155 (1 January 1970), p. 76.

Warrum, Richard L. Introduction to *Painting and Sculpture Today*. [Catalogue.] Indianapolis, Contemporary Art Society and Indianapolis Museum of Art, 1970.

Wellesley College Museum. "Jules Olitski." In *Contemporary Painting and Sculpture*, Wellesley, Jewett Art Center, 1970.

1971

Baker, Kenneth. "New York: Jules Olitski at Rubin Gallery, N.Y.." *Artforum*, vol. 9 (May 1971), p. 74.

"Ces douze peintres ont un point commun." *Connaissance des arts*, vol. 229 (March 1971), p. 132.

Domingo, Willis. "New York Galleries: Jules Olitski at Lawrence Rubin Gallery." *Arts Magazine*, vol. 45 (April 1971), p. 83.

Greenwood, Michael. "Jules Olitski's Sculpture." *Arts Canada*, vol. 28 (February–March 1971), p. 62.

Gruen, John. "While There's Life . . ." *New York Magazine*, 29 March 1971, p. 59.

Prokopoff, Stephen S. "Color Painting in America." *Art and Artists*, vol. 6 (July 1971), p. 22.

Ratcliff, Carter. "Reviews and Previews." *Art News*, vol. 70 (April 1971), p. 20.

Seigel, Jeanne. "Reviews and Previews: Jules Olitski." *Art News*, vol. 70 (September 1971), p. 17.

Tucker, Marcia. Essay in *The Structure of Color*. [Catalogue.] New York, Whitney Museum of American Art, 1971.

1972

Bannard, Walter Darby. "Quality, Style and Olitski." *Artforum*, vol. 11 (October 1972), pp. 64–67.

Carpenter, Ken. "On Order in the Paintings of Jules Olitski." *Art International*, vol. 16 (December 1972), pp. 26–30.

Elderfield, John. "Abstract Painting in the Seventies." *Art International*, vol. 16 (Summer 1972), pp. 92–94.

—. "Painterliness Redefined: Jules Olitski and Recent Abstract Art," Part I. *Art International*, vol. 16 (December 1972), pp. 22–25.

Matthias, Rosemary. "In the Galleries: Jules Olitski at Rubin." *Arts Magazine*, vol. 46 (Summer 1972), p. 56.

Moffett, Kenworth. Introduction to *Abstract Painting in the Seventies: A Selection*. [Catalogue.] Boston, Museum of Fine Arts, 1972.

Seigel, Jeanne. "Reviews and Previews: Jules Olitski." *Art News*, vol. 71 (Summer 1972), p. 56.

Wilkin, Karen. Introduction to *Masters of the Sixties*. [Catalogue.] Edmonton, Alberta, Edmonton Art Gallery, 1972.

Zemans, Joyce. "Olitski: The David Marvish Gallery." *Arts Canada*, vol. 29 (October–November 1972), p. 67.

47

8th Loosha, 1970, water-base acrylic on canvas, 115¼ x 68½ in. Courtesy Lawrence Rubin Gallery, New York.

48

3rd Indomitable, 1970, water-base acrylic on canvas, 83 x 216 in.
Private collection.

Catalogue

1

Demikov One, 1957, spackle, acrylic resin, and dry pigments on canvas, 37 x 37 in. Courtesy Lawrence Rubin Gallery, New York.

2

Triumph of Wentworth, 1958, spackle, acrylic resin, and dry pigments on canvas, 36¼ x 28⅞ in. Courtesy Lawrence Rubin Gallery, New York.

3

Molière's Chair II, 1959, spackle, acrylic resin, and dry pigments on canvas, 32½ x 32½ in. Collection of the artist.

4

Potsy, 1960, oil-miscible acrylic on canvas, 80 x 68¼ in. Courtesy Lawrence Rubin Gallery, New York.

5

House of Orange, ca. 1961–1962, oil-miscible acrylic on canvas, 80 x 91⅞ in. Courtesy Lawrence Rubin Gallery, New York.

6

After Five, 1961, acrylic resin on canvas, 92½ x 93½ in. Collection Mr. and Mrs. David Mirvish, Toronto.

7

Ino Delight, 1962, acrylic resin on canvas, 92 x 56 in. Norman Mackenzie Art Gallery, Regina.

8

Green Jazz, 1962, oil-miscible acrylic on canvas, 92 x 64 in. Collection J. Kasmin, London.

9

Born in Snovsk, 1963, oil-miscible acrylic on canvas, 132 x 90 in. The Art Institute of Chicago, Gift of the Ford Foundation.

10

Chemise, 1963, oil-miscible acrylic on canvas, 67 x 97½ in. Courtesy Lawrence Rubin Gallery, New York.

11

Fatal Plunge Lady, 1963, oil-miscible acrylic on canvas, 100 x 72 in. Kasmin Ltd., London.

12

V, 1963, oil-miscible acrylic on canvas, 64 x 64 in. Courtesy Lawrence Rubin Gallery, New York.

13

One Time, 1964, enamel paint on canvas, 82 x 69¼ in. Courtesy Lawrence Rubin Gallery, New York.

14

Monkey Woman, 1964, oil-miscible acrylic on canvas, 66 x 72 in. David Mirvish Gallery, Toronto.

15

Flaubert Red, 1964, oil-miscible acrylic on canvas, 82 x 106¾ in. Collection Rosalind Krauss, New York.

49

Radical Love–8, 1972, water-base acrylic on canvas, 98 x 42 in. Courtesy Lawrence Rubin Gallery, New York.

16
Tin Lizzy Green, 1964, oil-miscible acrylic on canvas,
115¼ x 68½ in. Courtesy Lawrence Rubin Gallery, New York.

17
Deep Drag, 1964, oil-miscible acrylic on canvas, 81½ x 118¼ in.
Collection Mr. and Mrs. Jack Lionel Warner, Santa Barbara.

18
Pink Shush, 1965, water-miscible acrylic on canvas, 79 x 66 in.
Private collection.

19
Bat, 1965, water-miscible acrylic on canvas, 108 x 72 in.
Kasmin Ltd., London.

20
Ariosto Kiss, 1965, water-miscible acrylic on canvas, 80¼ x 69 in.
Private collection.

21
Comprehensive Dream, 1965, water-miscible acrylic on canvas,
113 x 93 in. Collection Mr. and Mrs. Robert Rowan, Pasadena.

22
Sixth Caliph, 1965, water-miscible acrylic on canvas, 46 x 14¼ in.
Private collection.

23
Chinese Dinner, 1965, water-miscible acrylic on canvas,
18 x 54 in. Private collection.

24
Seize, 1966, water-miscible acrylic on canvas, 76 x 115 in.
Collection Mr. and Mrs. David Mirvish, Toronto.

25
Doulma, 1966, water-miscible acrylic on canvas, 68½ x 90 in.
Collection Mr. and Mrs. David Mirvish, Toronto.

26
Rexus, 1966, water-miscible acrylic on canvas, 92½ x 45 in.
Private collection.

27
Patutsky in Paradise, 1966, water-miscible acrylic on canvas,
115 x 162 in. Collection Susan and Ed Apfel, New York.

28
Pink Alert, 1966, water-miscible acrylic on canvas, 113 x 80 in.
The Corcoran Gallery of Art, Washington, D.C.

29
C + J & B, 1966, water-miscible acrylic on canvas, 69 x 115½ in.
Private collection.

30
Cross Spray, 1966, water-miscible acrylic on canvas, 89½ x 41 in.
Collection Mr. and Mrs. Harry W. Glasgall, New York.

52
Other Flesh–8, 1972, water-base acrylic on canvas, 86 x 51 in.
Collection Mr. and Mrs. Robert Rowan, Pasadena.

31

Free Departure, 1966, water-miscible acrylic on canvas,
114 x 84½ in. Private collection.

32

Unlocked, 1966, water-miscible acrylic on canvas, 140½ x 19 in.
Collection Robert Eichholz, Washington, D.C.

33

Thigh Smoke, 1966, water-miscible acrylic on canvas,
167 x 92½ in. Collection Seattle-First National Bank.

34

Beyond Bounds, 1966, water-miscible acrylic on canvas,
92½ x 62 in. Wellesley College Museum.

35

Pink Thrust, 1966, water-miscible acrylic on canvas, 115 x 42 in.
David Mirvish Gallery, Toronto.

36

End Run, 1967, water-miscible acrylic on canvas, 81 x 48 in.
Courtesy Lawrence Rubin Gallery, New York.

37

Lavender Liner, 1967, water-miscible acrylic on canvas,
65 x 180 in. Collection Kenneth Noland, New York.

38

Tender Boogus, 1967, water-miscible acrylic on canvas,
136¾ x 252½ in. Collection Mr. and Mrs. Robert Rowan, Pasadena.

39

Doessy, 1967, water-miscible acrylic on canvas, 51¾ x 19¾ in.
Courtesy Lawrence Rubin Gallery, New York.

40

Galliloo, 1967, water-miscible acrylic on canvas, 93½ x 43 in.
Courtesy Lawrence Rubin Gallery, New York.

41

Green Pressure, 1968, water-miscible acrylic on canvas,
118½ x 53½ in. Collection Kenneth Noland, New York.

42

Instant Loveland, 1968, water-miscible acrylic on canvas,
120 x 252 in. Kasmin Ltd., London.

43

Special Circumstances, 1968, water-miscible acrylic on canvas,
54 x 28 in. Private collection.

44

13th Hope, 1969, water-miscible acrylic on canvas, 60 x 22 in.
Courtesy Lawrence Rubin Gallery, New York.

45

Loosha–5, 1970, water-miscible acrylic on canvas, 72 x 24 in.
Private collection.

53

Call One, 1972, water-base acrylic on canvas, 89 x 105 in.
David Mirvish Gallery, Toronto.

46

Loosha–7, 1970, water-base acrylic on canvas, 107 x 68 in.
Private collection.

47

8th Loosha, 1970, water-base acrylic on canvas, 115¼ x 68½ in.
Courtesy Lawrence Rubin Gallery, New York.

48

3rd Indomitable, 1970, water-base acrylic on canvas, 83 x 216 in.
Private collection.

49

Radical Love–8, 1972, water-base acrylic on canvas, 98 x 42 in.
Courtesy Lawrence Rubin Gallery, New York.

50

Embarked I, 1972, water-base acrylic on canvas, 92 x 60 in.
David Mirvish Gallery, Toronto.

51

Other Flesh–1, 1972, water-base acrylic on canvas, 100 x 68 in.
Collection of the artist.

52

Other Flesh–8, 1972, water-base acrylic on canvas, 86 x 51 in.
Collection Mr. and Mrs. Robert Rowan, Pasadena.

53

Call One, 1972, water-base acrylic on canvas, 89 x 105 in.
David Mirvish Gallery, Toronto.

54

Other Flesh–11, 1972, water-base acrylic on canvas, 82 x 66 in.
David Mirvish Gallery, Toronto.

55

5th Omsk, 1972, water-base acrylic on canvas, 120 x 24 in.
Private collection.

56

Radical Love–19, 1972, water-base acrylic on canvas, 69 x 50 in.
Courtesy Lawrence Rubin Gallery, New York.

57

Radical Love–20, 1972, water-base acrylic on canvas, 100 x 79 in.
Collection Mr. and Mrs. R. Davidson, Toronto.

58

First Front, 1972, water-base acrylic on canvas, 80 x 62 in.
Courtesy Lawrence Rubin Gallery, New York.

59

Radical Love–28, 1972, water-base acrylic on canvas, 14 x 68 in.
Collection Dawn Andrews, New York.

60

Fourth Front, 1972, water-base acrylic on canvas, 74 x 65 in.
Collection of the artist.

57

Radical Love–20, 1972, water-base acrylic on canvas, 100 x 79 in.
Collection Mr. and Mrs. R. Davidson, Toronto.